Land Developer's
Checklists and Forms

Land Developer's Checklists and Forms

R. Dodge Woodson

McGraw-Hill

New York Chicago San Francisco Lisbon London Madrid
Mexico City Milan New Delhi San Juan Seoul
Singapore Sydney Toronto

I dedicate this book to my daughter, Afton, and my son, Adam.
The two of them are my focus in life.

Acknowledgments

I wish to thank the state, federal, and local agencies who have provided some of the illustrations for this book. Additionally, I want to acknowledge Victoria Roberts for her diligent work in obtaining the art from these agencies and organizing it for me.

About the Author

R. Dodge Woodson has been involved in real estate speculation for over 30 years. He holds the license of a Designated Broker, the highest classification of a real estate license available. In addition to being a broker and the owner of Expert Realty Services, Inc., Woodson is a homebuilder. He has built as many as 60 homes per year. His building company, The Masters Group, Inc., is known for its quality, ethics, and dependability. Simply put, Woodson has spent his life in real estate and construction. When it comes to residential land development, Woodson's combined experience as a developer and builder is hard to match.

Preface

Land development can be a very lucrative venture. But, the road to success can have many pitfalls. Anyone can use some help from time to time, and this resource is exactly the type of help that any residential land developer can benefit from.

As you thumb through these pages you will find many types of forms and examples of information to make your job easier, faster, and more profitable. And, unlike many books, the forms in this book are available online for your use. To access these forms electronically, go to www.MHEngineeringResouces.com and follow the instructions on the site.

With this book and the available electronic files, your odds of success increase dramatically. Would you like another boost to your career? Check out Woodson's other book, *Be a Successful Residential Land Developer*. When you have both books and the online forms, you should be all set to become a developer.

Table of Contents

Chapter 6
Working With Contractors 131

Chapter 7
Managing Your Development 191

Introduction

Becoming a land developer can mean making a lot of money. And, you don't have to use a lot of your own cash to break into the business. Of course, the more money you have, the easier the task will be. Money is needed, and sometimes a lot of money is needed, but you can work with loans or partners to avoid tapping too hard into your own savings.

It is not unusual for land developers to double their money when they turn raw land into building lots. Any homebuilder should consider developing building lots. The additional money made from the sale of a home that is built on a lot that you developed can be substantial.

Not all land is suitable for development. You may find parcels that are in a flood plain. This can be a problem, but it may not be a deal-stopper. A full investigation is warranted for any piece of land that shows strong potential.

This book is designed to introduce you to the many elements of paperwork involved with developing land. My other book, *Be a Successful Residential Land Developer*, goes into great depth on the procedures for becoming a profitable developer. This book is the ideal companion title in that it gives you visual examples of the types of forms, checklists, and applications that you are likely to be exposed to as a developer.

There are a number of professionals who will prove to be quite helpful to you during your development procedures. If you have good organizational skills and a knack for being self-disciplined, you have a good chance of making a go of being a land developer. The experts who you surround yourself with will make the technical work easier.

When you are planning a project, you will need site plans and sketches. Your stable of professionals can take care of this for you. Engineers and surveyors will do much of the work. These people are expensive, but they are essential to a strong development. The key factor is that you don't have to possess any particular strength to learn how to develop land.

What types of lots will you develop? Is a building lot just a building lot? Not at all. There are many different types of subdivisions and, within those subdivisions, there are various types of lots. You must decide how to lay out roadways. A lot of land can be lost to road construction. There is much to learn before you buy land for a development project. The principles laid out in this book apply to all types of residential land development.

If you are serious about becoming a successful land developer, you need this book and my previous book, *Be a Successful Residential Land Developer*. Just thumb through these pages and look for yourself at all the forms, checklists, and sample agreements that are contained within these pages. Where else can you find real-world examples of what you are likely to deal with as a developer? The information here is real. I use these forms myself, and the sample applications are real. Getting familiar with the paperwork before you are faced with it during your project will certainly save you time and frustration, not to mention the potential of saving money at the same time.

Should You Become a Land Developer?

- Are you already a homebuilder? If so, developing can enhance your income considerably.

- Do you enjoy a flexible schedule, even if it can be demanding? Becoming a developer can give you a lot of freedom and strong income, but the hours invested can be far more than 40 hours a week.

- Are you well organized? You will need to be if you want to be successful as a developer.

- Are you willing to invest/risk your money to establish a development? It's possible to work with small sums of money, but many projects require tens of thousands of dollars to get started.

- Should I consider working with partners? If you need financial help, partners may be the answer. The right marriage of partners can improve your odds of success. For example, if you are a developer and you bring in a partner who owns a real estate brokerage and a partner who is a homebuilder, you might do very well.

- How much risk is involved with land development? There is always risk, and developing land can carry substantial risk with it. But, the reward potential is also significant.

- Does it take a long time to become a developer? A small project can be developed in less than a year. Larger projects can take several years to develop.

- How will I learn about zoning, soil studies, and stuff like that? You will build a team of experienced professionals who will work with you.

- How much money will I make? It's not uncommon for developers to sell finished projects for twice what they paid for the land. There are expenses, but the money can be tremendous.

Figure I-1 Should you become a land developer?

Helpful Traits for Becoming a Land Developer

- Are you creative? Ideas are a big part of success as a developer. If you can look at situations and see beyond them, you have a good chance of winning as a developer.

- Having money, good credit, or a stable full of associates who can assist in monetary matters is always helpful. Depending on the size and type of project you are interested in, you will not need a huge amount of money, but developing land is not a cheap proposition.

- Organizational skills are essential if you are going to run your own projects. If you are lacking in this area, consider hiring a project manager.

- Research is one of the best tools for keeping yourself out of trouble as a developer. If you can dig deep and compile extensive research on potential projects, your odds of success shoot way up.

- People skills are needed to make project development enjoyable. If you are not good with people, consider hiring a field superintendent to handle meetings and management.

- Time is always a factor in developing land. Moving too slowly can mean increasing interest rates that will crush your profit projects. On the other hand, you can take years to develop land without losing money. Time is flexible in this field of work.

Figure I-2 Helpful traits for becoming a land developer

Experts Worth Knowing

There are many potential experts needed in land development projects. A brief listing of some experts who may come in handy includes:

- Attorneys will be needed. This may include real estate attorneys and tax attorneys.

- Certified public accountants are essential when it comes to evaluating tax advantages and consequences for a project.

- Marketing consultants are often used on large projects, but they are rarely needed on small jobs.

- Homebuilders add a great dimension to most development deals.

- Project planners, field superintendents, and project managers are all worth building good relations with.

- Architects, both structural and landscaping, may be needed.

- Civil engineers are almost always an asset to a project.

- Surveyors are typically an essential need for any project.

- Geologists may be required for your project.

- Real estate brokers

- Many other types of experts can add to the value of your project.

Figure I-3   Experts worth knowing

Types of Subdivisions

- Conventional subdivisions

- Cluster subdivisions

- Planned unit development (PUDs)

- Planned community

- Master-planned community

Figure I-4   Types of subdivisions

Types of Building Lots

- Single-family detached lots

- Conventional building lots

- Cluster building lots

- Pie-shaped lots

- Pipe-stem-shaped lots

- Flag-shaped lots

- Zero-lot-line lots

- Z lots

- Angled Z lots

- Squat lots

- Side-shallow lots

- Wide-shallow lots

- Single-family, semi-detached lots

- Single-family, attached lots

- Townhouse lots

- Back-to-back townhouse lots

- Stacked townhouse lots

- Piggyback townhouse lots

- Multiplex lots

- Multifamily residential lots

- Garden-style apartment lots

- Mid-rise multifamily lots

- High-rise multifamily lots

Figure I-5 Types of building lots

Road Design Considerations

- Alignment of roads and streets

- Cul-de-sacs

- Looping streets

- Environmental impact

- Land lost due to road construction

- Double-loaded streets

- Avoiding excessive street length

- Signage requirements

- Soil conditions

- Medians

- Shoulders

- Utilities

- Road width

- Road bed compaction

- Entry points from lots to roads and streets

- Blind spots

- Safe turnarounds

- Provisions for snow removal

Figure I-6   Road design considerations

Chapter 1

Financial Budgets and Considerations

Money moves the business climate. Anyone who has been involved in land development knows the value of money and credit. While it cannot be said that you will fail as a developer without money, a developer who is without money or credit is at an extreme disadvantage. Land development is difficult enough with money, and without cash, the hurdles become higher.

You can use other people's money when you are not properly funded. But, this can get complicated. It is better to control your own deck of cards when you are betting the odds. Therefore, establishing viable budgets and presenting your lenders with convincing proposals should be high on your to-do list. This chapter will show you some sample forms that will be very helpful in the financial factors of a development project.

Budget Information—Construction Programs

OMB Approval No. 0348-0041

Note: Certain Federal assistance programs require additional computations to arrive at the Federal share of project costs eligible for participation. If such is the case you will be notified.

Cost Classification	a. Total Cost	b. Costs Not Allowable for Participation	c. Total Allowable Costs (Column a-b)
1. Administrative and legal expenses	$ .00	$ .00	$ .00
2. Land, structures, rights-of-way, appraisals, etc.	$ .00	$ .00	$ .00
3. Relocation expenses and payments	$ .00	$ .00	$ .00
4. Architectural and engineering fees	$ .00	$ .00	$ .00
5. Other architectural and engineering fees	$ .00	$ .00	$ .00
6. Project inspection fees	$ .00	$ .00	$ .00
7. Site work	$ .00	$ .00	$ .00
8. Demolition and removal	$ .00	$ .00	$ .00
9. Construction	$ .00	$ .00	$ .00
10. Equipment	$ .00	$ .00	$ .00
11. Miscellaneous	$ .00	$ .00	$ .00
12. **Subtotal**	$ .00	$ .00	$ .00
13. Contingencies (sum of lines 1-11)	$ .00	$ .00	$ .00
14. **Subtotal**	$ .00	$ .00	$ .00
15. Project (program) income	$ .00	$ .00	$ .00
16. **Total Project Costs** (subtract #15 from #14)	$ .00	$ .00	$ .00

Federal Funding

17. Federal assistance requested, calculate as follows: Enter eligible costs from line 16c _____ Multiply x _____ %
(Consult Federal agency for Federal percentage share).
Enter the resulting Federal share. .... $ _____ .00

Previous Edition Usable

Page 1 of 2
Authorized for Local Reproduction

SF-424C (Rev. 4/92)
Prescribed by OMB Circular A-102

Figure 1.1   Sample of a budget form for construction programs *(continued on next page)*

Instructions for HUD-424C

Public reporting burden for this collection of information is estimated to average 3 hours per response, including the time for reviewing instructions, searching existing data sources, gathering and maintaining the data needed, and completing and reviewing the collection of information. Send comments regarding this burden estimate or any other aspect of this collection of information, including suggestions for reducing this burden to the Office of Management and Budget, Paperwork Reduction Project (0348-0041), Washington, D.C. 20503. Please do not return your completed form to the Office of Management and Budget; send it to the address provided by the sponsoring agency.

This sheet is to be used for the following types of applications: (1) "New" (means a new [previously unfunded[assistance award); (2) "Continuation" (means funding in a succeeding budget period which stemmed from a prior agreement to fund); and (3) "Revised" (means any changes in the Federal government's financial obligations or contingent liability from an existing obligation). If there is no change in the award amount there is no need to complete this form. Certain Federal agencies may require only an explanatory letter to effect minor (no cost) changes. If you have questions please contact the Federal agency.

Column a.—If this is an application for a "New" project, enter the total estimated cost of each of the items listed on lines 1 through 16 (as applicable) under "**Cost Classifications.**"

If this application entails a change to an existing award, enter the eligible amounts **approved under the previous award** for the items under "**Cost Classification.**"

Column b.—If this is an application for a "New" project, enter that portion of the cost of each item in Column a. which is **not** allowable for Federal assistance. Contact the Federal agency for assistance in determining the allowability of specific costs.

If this application entails a change to an existing award, enter the adjustment [+ or (−)] to the previously approved costs (from column a.) reflected in this application.

Column c.—This is the net of lines 1 through 16 in columns "a." and "b.".

Line 1—Enter estimated amounts needed to cover administrative expenses. Do not include costs which are related to the normal functions of government. Allowable legal costs are generally only those associated with the purchase of land which is allowable for Federal participation and certain services in support of construction of the project.

Line 2—Enter estimated site and right(s)-of-way acquisition costs (this includes purchase, lease, and/or easements).

Line 3—Enter estimated costs related to relocation advisory assistance, replacement housing, relocation payments to displaced persons and businesses, etc.

Line 4—Enter estimated basic engineering fees related to construction (this includes start-up services and preparation of project performance work plan).

Line 5—Enter estimated engineering costs, such as surveys, tests, soil borings, etc.

Line 6—Enter estimated engineering inspection costs.

Line 7—Enter estimated costs of site preparation and restoration which are not included in the basic construction contract.

Line 9—Enter estimated cost of the construction contract.

Line 10—Enter estimated cost of office, shop, laboratory, safety equipment, etc. to be used at the facility, if such costs are not included in the construction contract.

Line 11—Enter estimated miscellaneous costs.

Line 12—Total of items 1 through 11.

Line 13—Enter estimated contingency costs. (Consult the Federal agency for the percentage of the estimated construction cost to use.)

Line 14—Enter the total of lines 12 and 13.

Line 15—Enter estimated program income to be earned during the grant period, e.g., salvaged materials, etc.

Line 16—Subtract line 15 from line 14.

Item 17—This block is for the computation of the Federal share. Multiply the total allowable project costs from line 16, column "c." by the Federal percentage share (this may be up to 100 percent; consult Federal agency for Federal percentage share) and enter the product on line 17.

SF-424C (Rev. 4/92)
Prescribed by OMB Circular A-102

Page 2 of 2
Authorized for Local Reproduction

Figure 1.1 *(continued from previous page)* Sample of a budget form for construction programs

USDA-RD
Form RD 442-7
(Rev. 3-02)

Position 3

OPERATING BUDGET

Form Approved
OMB No. 0575-0015

Schedule 1

Name		Address		
Applicant Fiscal Year		County	State *(Including ZIP Code)*	
From	To			

	20____ (1)	20____ (2)	20____ (3)	20____ (4)	First Full Year (5)
OPERATING INCOME					
1._____					
2._____					
3._____					
4._____					
5. Miscellaneous					
6. Less: Allowances and Deductions	( )	( )	( )	( )	( )
7. Total Operating Income *(Add Lines 1 through 6)*					
OPERATING EXPENSES					
8._____					
9._____					
10._____					
11._____					
12._____					
13._____					
14._____					
15. Interest *(RD)*					
16. Depreciation					
17. Total Operating Expense *(Add Lines 8 through 16)*					
18. NET OPERATING INCOME *(LOSS) (Line 7 less 17)*					
NONOPERATING INCOME					
19._____					
20._____					
21. Total Nonoperating Income *(Add Lines 19 and 20)*					
22. NET INCOME *(LOSS) (Add Lines 18 and 21) (Transfer to Line A Schedule 2)*					

Budget and Projected Cash Flow Approved by Governing Body

Attest: _____   _____
                              Secretary   *Date*

_____   _____
Appropriate Official   *Date*

Figure 1.2 An operating budget form *(continued on next page)*

PROJECTED CASH FLOW   Schedule 2

	20_____	20_____	20_____	20_____	First Full Year
A. Line 22 from Schedule 1 Income *(Loss)*					
Add					
B. Items in Operations not Requiring Cash:					
1. Depreciation *(Line 16, Schedule 1)*					
2. Others: _____					
C. Cash Provided from:					
1. Proceeds from RD loan/grant					
2. Proceeds from others					
3. Increase *(Decrease)* in Accounts Payable, Accurals and other Current Liabilities					
4. Decrease *(Increase)* in Accounts Receivable, Inventories and Other Current Assets *(Exclude Cash)*					
5. Other: _____					
6. _____					
D. Total all A, B, and C Items					
E. *Less:* Cash Expended for:					
1. All Construction, Equipment and New Capital Items *(Loan and grant funds)*					
2. Replacement and Additions to Existing Property, Plant and Equipment					
3. Principal Payment RD Loan					
4. Principal Payment Other Loans					
5. Other: _____					
6. Total E 1 through 5					
Add					
F. Beginning Cash Balances					
G. Ending Cash Balances *(Total of D minus E 6 plus F)*					
Item G Cash Balance Composed of:	$	$	$	$	$
Construction Account					
Revenue Account					
Debt Payment Account	$	$	$	$	$
O&M Account					
Reserve Account					
Funded Depreciation Account					
Others: _____					
Total - Agrees with Item G	$	$	$	$	$

Figure 1.2 *(continued from previous page)* An operating budget form

Instructions - Operating Budget Schedule 1

This form is to be prepared by the Applicant and is to include data for each year, from loan closing through the first full year of operation. Example: If only two columns are required, use columns four(4) and five(5).

Income and Expense Items:

All data entered should be on the same basis as the Applicant's Accounting records, i.e., cash basis, accrual basis, etc.

Operating Income:

lines 1-5   List types of income as appropriate
line 6 —   Allowances and Deductions
            (Pertains generally to Health Care Institutions, and represents the difference between Gross Income and Amounts Received or to be Received from patients and third party payors)

Operating Expenses:

lines 8-14 List types of expenses as appropriate
line 15 —   Interest RD
            (Interest expense incurred on RD note(s))
line 16 —   Depreciation
            (Total depreciation expense for the year)
line 18—   Net Operating (Loss)
            (This amount represents the net operating income or loss before adding income not related to operations below)

Non Operating Income:

lines 19-20 Indicate items of income derived from sources other than regular activities
            (Example: interest earned)
line 22 —   Net income *(Loss)*
            (This amount is also transferred to item A, Schedule 2, Projected Cash Flow Statement)

Instructions - Projected Cash Flow, Schedule 2

This from is used to Project the flow of Cash by the Applicant for each year, from loan closing through the first full year of operation. Use the same number of columns as used on the Operating Budget, Schedule 1. These Cash Flow Projections are important in determining the adequacy of cash to cover operating expenses, transfers to debt payment, reserve accounts, etc.

Cash Basis Accounting

Applicants who maintain their records strictly on the cash basis of accounting and have no Accounts Receivable and Accounts Payable, may only need to complete the following line items: A, B-1, C-1, E-1 and E-3, F and G.

Line Item Instructions:

line A —   Bring forward the income or loss as entered on line 22, Schedule 1.
line B —   Add back any depreciation or other non cash items included on Schedule 1, Operating Budget.
line C —   Complete items C-1 through C-6 as appropriate, for item changes which provide for increase in cash balances.
           NOTE: Do not include changes in cash Accounts in Current Assets of item C4. Lines C-3 and C-4 will indicate the changes in Working Capital *(Current Assets and Current Liabilities, Exclusive of Cash.)*
line D —   Enter the Net Total of all A, B and C items.
line E —   complete items E-1 through E-6 as appropriate for items for which cash was expended.
line F —   Enter the Beginning Cash Balance(s) for the period.
line G —   The total of item D less E-6 plus F will be the Ending Cash Balance(s). The total will be reconciled by balances in the various accounts, i.e., construction, revenue, debt, etc.

Figure 1.2   *(continued from previous page)* An operating budget form

Development Cost Budget/ Cost Statement

U.S. Department of Housing and Urban Development
Office of Public and Indian Housing

OMB Approval No. 2577-0036 (exp. 5/31/2004)

Dwelling Units			Copy Number:		PR/Project Number:
Family	Elderly	Total			
			Public Housing Agency:		Locality of Project:

No financial or technical assistance may be provided to a project pursuant to an Annual Contributions Contract unless a PHA Proposal, including a development cost budget, has been approved (24 CFR 941).

Housing Type and Production Method	Turnkey	Conv.	Force Act.
New Construction			
ACQ W/Subst. Rehab.			
ACQ WO/Subst. Rehab.			

Status (Check one)
- [ ] Budget Between PP and Contract Award
- [ ] Contract of Sale/Contract Award Budget
- [ ] Budget Between Contract Award & Final

- [ ] PHA Proposal (PP) Budget
- [ ] Final Development Cost Budget
- [ ] Development Cost Control Statement
- [ ] Statement of Actual Development Cost

Subpart I - Budget

Line No.	Account Classification (a)	Latest Approved Budget Date _____ (b)	Actual Development Cost Incurred To _____ (c)	Actual Contract Award Balance (d)	Estimated Additional to Complete (e)	Amount (c) + (d) + (e) (f)	Per Unit (g)
Developer's Price							
1	1440 Site						
2	1450 Site Improvements						
3	1460 Dwelling Construction						
4	1465 Dwelling Equipment						
5	1470 Nondwelling Construction						
6	1475 Nondwelling Equipment						
7	1430.1 Archit. & Engr. Svcs.						
8	Other						
9	**Total Developer's Price**						
Public Housing Agency Costs							
Operations							
10	1406 Operations						
Administration							
11	1410.1 Nontechnical Salaries						
12	1410.2 Technical Salaries						
13	1410.4 Legal Expenses						
14	1410.9 Employee Benefit Contribution						
15	1410.10 Travel						
16	1410.18 Equipment Expended						
17	1410.19 Sundry						
18	**Total Administration**						
Liquidated Damages							
19	1415 Liquidated Damages						
Interest							
20	1420.1 Interest to HUD						
21	1420.2 Interest on Notes—Non-HUD						
22	1420.7 Interest Earned from Invest.						
23	**Total Interest**						
Initial Operating Deficit							
24	1425 Initial Operating Deficit						
Planning							
25	1430.1 Architectural & Engr. Fees						
26	1430.2 Consultant Fees						
27	1430.6 Permit Fees						
28	1430.7 Inspection Costs						
29	1430.9 Housing Surveys						
30	1430.19 Sundry Planning Costs						
31	**Total Planning**						

form **HUD-52484** (8/96)
ref Handbook 7417.1

Figure 1.3 Development cost budget and cost statement *(continued on next page)*

Copy Number:			PR/Project Number:			

Subpart I - Budget (continued)

Line No.	Account Classification (a)	Latest Approved Budget Date _____ (b)	Actual Development Cost Incurred To _____ (c)	Actual Contract Award Balance (d)	Estimated Additional to Complete (e)	Amount (c) + (d) + (e) (f)	Per Unit (g)
	Site Acquisition						
32	1440.1 Property Purchases						
33	1440.2 Condemnation Deposits						
34	1440.3 Excess Property						
35	1440.4 Surveys and Maps						
36	1440.5 Appraisals						
37	1440.6 Title Information						
38	1440.8 Legal Costs – Site						
39	1440.10 Option Negotiations						
40	1440.12 Current Tax Settlement						
41	1440.19 Sundry Site Costs						
42	1440.20 Site Net Income						
43	**Total Site Acquisition**						
44	1450 **Site Improvements**						
45	1460 **Dwelling Construction**						
46	1465 **Dwelling Equipment**						
47	1470 **Nondwelling Construction**						
48	1475 **Nondwelling Equipment**						
49	1480 **Contract Work in Progress**						
50	1485 **Demolition**						
51	1495 **Relocation Costs**						
52	1499 **Development Used for Mod.**						
53	**Total** (Including Donations)						
54	Less Donations						
55	**Total Before Contingency** (less Donations)						
56	Contingency: 1% to 5% (or less) of line 55						
57	**Total Development Cost**						

Subpart II - Detail of Other in Developer's Price

1. Developer's Fee and Overhead $ _____
2. Interim Financing   _____
3. Closing Costs   _____
4. Property Taxes and Assessments   _____
5. State or Local Sales, Excise or Other Taxes   _____

    Total Other $ _____

Subpart III - Supporting Data for Cost Estimates

For the PP Budget, attach an itemized breakdown of the costs chargeable to each of the following accounts. For subsequent budgets, provide this information only for accounts that are being changed.

1410.1 and 1410.2: List, by job title, each PHA employee whose salary, or portions thereof, will be chargeable to these accounts. For each, show the annual rate of gross salary, the estimated length of time to be spent in connection with development of this project, and the total gross salary which is properly chargeable to either of these accounts. If only a portion of the employee's time will be chargeable to this project, show the percentage that will be so chargeable; and show, in a footnote, the percentage distribution to other projects and the accounts to which distributed.

1410.19: List and show the cost of each item of administrative and general expense for which a specific account is not provided in the 1410 group of accounts. If only a portion of the cost of any item will be chargeable to this project, show the percentage and amount that will be so chargeable; and show, in a footnote, the percentage distribution to other projects.

1430.2: List all planning consultants not paid under the architect's contract and, for each, identify and show the cost of the services provided.

1430.7: Provide the same information required for 1410.1 and 1410.2, listing employees of the architect (or PHA when use of PHA employees has been previously approved) who will perform inspection work for the project.

1450: Where off-site facilities are proposed to be included, identify and show the cost of such facilities and provide justification for including such costs in TDC.

1465: Identify and show the cost of each item included in this account.

1475: Complete the Table below and, on a separate attachment, list and show the cost of each item included in each sub-account.

Nondwelling Equipment (1475)	Cost
1475.1 Office Furniture and Equipment	
1475.2 Maintenance Equipment	
1475.3 Community Space Equipment	
1475.7 Automotive Equipment	
1475.9 Expendable Equipment	
Total Nonswelling Equipment	

1495: State the number of households and businesses to be displaced, and identify and show the estimated cost of relocation services and payments to be provided.

form **HUD-52484** (8/96)
ref Handbook 7417.1

Figure 1.3 *(continued from previous page)* Development cost budget and cost statement

Copy Number: _____

PR/Project Number: _____

Subpart IV - New Construction – Prototype Cost Comparison Percentage

A. Dwelling Construction and Equipment (DC&E) Cost from Subpart I

   1. Total for Account 1460 $ _____

   2. Total for Account 1465   _____

   3. Subtotal (1 + 2) $ _____

   4. Contingency (_____% x line 3)   _____

   5. Total DC&E (3 + 4) $ _____

B. PPCL Total   _____

   (Attach calculation from PP, Part I, Subpart B, Item 3)

C. Comparison Percentage   = _____ %

   (Line A5 ÷ Line B)

Subpart V - Acquisition–Development Cost Comparison Percentage

A. Proposed TDC from Subpart I $ _____

B. Hypothetical TDC $ _____

   (Attach calculation from PP, Part I,

   Subpart B, Item 5a or, if applicable,

   other estimate and rationale.)

C. Comparison Percentage   = _____ %

   (Line A ÷ Line B)

Subpart VI - Detail of Donations

Line No.	Item (Please List)	Amount (Value)
1		
2		
3		
4		
	Total	

Subpart VII - Previously Approved Budgets

List chronologically the dates and TDC on all previously approved budgets, beginning with the PHA Proposal (P) Budget, and state the purpose (i.e., one of the budgets listed in the "Status" block on page 1 and any amendments thereto).

Date	TDC	Purpose
		PP

I hereby certify that all the information stated herein, as well as any information provided in the accompaniment herewith, is true and accurate.

Warning: HUD will prosecute false claims and statements. Conviction may result in criminal and/or civil penalties. (18 U.S.C. 1001, 1010, 1012; 31 U.S.C. 3729, 3802)

Submitted By: Name & Title of Official Authorized to Sign for PHA:

Signature of PHA's Authorized Official & Date:

X

For HUD Use Only

Recommended for Approval By: Name & Title of Authorized Official:

Signature of Authorized Official & Date:

X

Approved By: Name & Title of Authorized Official:

Signature of Authorized Official & Date:

X

form **HUD-52484** (8/96)
ref Handbook 7417.1

Figure 1.3 *(continued from previous page)* Development cost budget and cost statement

This form HUD-52484 includes the account classification numbers, actual development cost incurred, actual contract award balance, and total development cost which are apart of a Public Housing Agency's (PHA's) development cost budget/cost statement for development of a public housing project.

PHAs provide information on the amount of monies which will be needed to develop the project and other costs associated with it . The information collected in the proposal is used by HUD for review and approval of development funds.

Public Reporting Burden for this collection of information is estimated to average 10 hours per response, including the time for reviewing instructions, searching existing data sources, gathering and maintaining the data needed, and completing and reviewing the collection of information.

Response to this collection of information is mandatory to obtain a benefit or to retain a benefit.

The information requested does not lend itself to confidentiality.

HUD may not conduct or sponsor, and person is not required to respond to a collection of information unless it displays a currently valid OMB control number.

Instructions for Preparing Development Cost Budgets/Cost Statements, Form HUD-52484

A. General

This form HUD-52484 shall be used for all Development Cost Budgets and Statements identified in the "Status" section on page 1 and should be carefully completed for each type of submission. For information supplementing these instructions, see Public Housing Development Handbook 7417.1 Descriptions of the budget accounts to which costs should be charged are set forth in Low-Rent Technical Accounting Guide 7510.1, Chapter 4, Section 15. The HUD Field Office, upon request, will assist PHAs in the distribution of costs to individual accounts.

1. **General Preparation.** The Form should cover all of the housing to be built under a single Contract of Sale/Construction Contract, whether on one or several sites. The "Dwelling Units" section at the top of page 1 shall show, in the "Elderly" block, the total of all units designed specifically for the elderly, including any such units which have more than one bedroom; and the other sections at the top of the page shall be completed as appropriate. Round out all amounts to even dollars. Where descriptions or supplementary data are required, use an attached sheet, identifying the item to which it is applicable.

I hereby certify that all the information stated herein, as well as any information provided in the accompaniment herewith, is true and accurate. **Warning:** HUD will prosecute false claims and statements. Conviction may result in criminal and/or civil penalties. (18 U.S.C. 1001, 1010, 1012; 31 U.S.C. 3729, 3802)

2. **Use of Form as Development Cost Budget**

a. When first used (with form HUD-52483-A, PHA Proposal (PP), Part I, Subpart B, Item 2), the PHA shall submit an original and 2 copies to the HUD Field Office, as in the case of the PP and other related attachments. (If any major changes are proposed following approval of the PP, a revised PP and PP budget shall be submitted in accordance with Handbook 7417.1.) If there was no preliminary loan, the PHA shall enter the estimated costs for development of the project in column (f) and complete column (g) as appropriate. If the PHA received a preliminary loan, the form shall be completed as follows. In column (b), cross out the words "Latest Approved Budget" in the heading and enter the date the Preliminary Loan Contract was executed; enter the words "Preliminary Loan Contract" lengthwise in the column; and enter the total preliminary loan amount in line 58. In columns (c) and (d), enter the latest readily available figures from the books of account maintained for the Preliminary Loan Contract; and, in the heading of column (c), enter the date as of which such figures were taken. In column (e), enter the estimated costs for development of the project. Enter in column (f) the sum of columns (c), (d) and (e); and complete column (g) as appropriate.

b. For subsequent Development Cost Budgets, submit an original and 2 copies to the HUD Field Office. Enter the date of the latest approved budget in the heading of column (b) and, for each line item, enter the applicable latest approved cost. Enter in columns (c) and (d) the latest readily available figures from the books of account for Accounts 1410 through 1475 and Accounts 1485, 1495, and 1499; and, in the heading of column (c), show the date as of which such figures were taken. Enter in column (e) for each Account 1410 through 1475, 1485, 1495, and 1499 an estimate of any additional cost to be incurred in completing the development work. Enter in column (v) the sum of columns (c), (d) and (e); and complete column (g) as appropriate. For Account 1480, which is not applicable to turnkey projects, leave all columns blank until submission of the Contract Award Budget. At that time and thereafter, the entries for Account 1480 shall be as follows:

(1) For a Contract Award Budget, list each proposed construction contract to be included under Account 1480 in column (a) by name of contractor and type of work. Opposite each such listing, enter in columns (d) and (f) the amount shown in column (3) of the corresponding form HUD-52396, Analysis of Main Construction Contact (or, in cases where a change in any bid amount is proposed, enter the amount shown in column (5) of form HUD-52396 and identify change order(s) included in the contract amount). Amounts for all work and equipment not covered by contracts shall remain in the appropriate subsidiary account.

(2) For each budget submitted after a Contract Award Budget, enter in column (c) the total of payments made to each contractor; in column (d) the balance owing under each original contract; in column (e) the amount of any increases or decreases for change orders known to be needed at the time the budget is submitted; and in column (f) the sum of columns (c), (d) and (e). If the sum of columns (c) and (d) differs from the original contract amount in column (f) of the latest approved budget because of executed change orders, identify such change orders.

(3) For the Final Budget, this Account 1480 is to be left blank and the amounts for each completed construction contract shall be redistributed to the appropriate Accounts 1450 through 1475, 1485, and 1499. On an attachment to the Final Budget, identify each construction contract by name of contractor and type of work; and show the final contract amounts, broken down in to the appropriate Accounts 1450 through 1475, 1485, and 1499.

3. **Use of Form as Cost Statement**

a. When used as the quarterly Development Cost Control Statement (required during the period beginning with the date a project is placed under an ACC and ending with the date the form HUD-52427, Actual Development Cost Certificate, is submitted for each project), columns (b), (c), (d) and (f) shall be completed; and columns (e) and (g) shall be left blank. However, in cases where the PHA is reasonably certain that it will be necessary to incur additional costs that were not anticipated at the time of submission of the latest approved budget (identified in column (b)), the PHA shall enter the estimated amounts of such additional costs in column (e) so the Field Office will be aware of its budgetary problems and can take appropriate steps to help solve them. (In such cases, the amount in column (f) will be the sum of columns (c), (d) and (e).) If

form **HUD-52484** (8/96)
ref Handbook 7417.1

Figure 1.3 *(continued from previous page)* Development cost budget and cost statement

it is determined that the solution involves a change in any of the latest approved budget amounts, the PHA shall prepare a revised budget and submit it to the Field Office in accordance with instructions in Handbook 7417.1 and Item A2b, above.

b. When used as the Statement of Actual Development Cost (which is submitted simultaneously with form HUD-52427, Actual Development Cost Certificate), only columns (b) and (c) shall be completed for all accounts, except Account 1480 (which requires no entries in any column).

B. Subpart I – Budget

1. Development Method

a. **Turnkey.** For projects developed under the turnkey method, the account classifications for Developer's Price (lines 1 through 9) are to be completed. Where preselected sites are used, entries should be made in lines 32 through 43, as applicable, for those site costs borne by the PHA prior to the assignment to the developer of the right to purchase the site. The Total Developer's Price (line 9) shall be the price agreed upon by the developer, the PHA and HUD. The amounts entered for site and architectural and engineering services (lines 1 and 7) should be the amounts to be included, where applicable, in the Preliminary Contract of Sale for the eventuality of separate purchase by he PHA. The amount entered for Other (line 98 and Subpart II) should be the sum of (1) Developer's fee and Overhead, exclusive of builder-contractor's overhead and profit which is in other items of the developer's price; (2) Interim Financing; (3) Closing Costs; (4) property taxes and assessments during construction; and (5) State or local sales, excise or other taxes, if any. Planning costs approved by the HUD Field Office will allow for entries in lines 25 and 26, as well as in line 7 (in addition to inspections for which an entry will be made in line 28).

b. **Conventional.** For conventional projects, lines 1 through 9 will remain blank and, instead, those accounts will be completed utilizing lines 25 through 48. For lines 44 through 48, the Schematic Design Documents and the Architect's Estimate of Project Construction Cost will provide a basis for reasonable estimates for costs. Any comments from the HUD Field Office as a result of the prior submission of these documents shall be reflected in the Budget.

c. **Acquisition.** For acquisition projects, Account 1440 will be the approved price for the site, including the structures thereon which are to be acquired for the project; and Accounts 1450 through 1485 will be used for the work to be done. Lines 1 through 9, or 32 through 48, will be completed as required by the development method being used and other instructions herein.

2. 1410 – Administration (lines 10 through 18).
PHAs with experience in the development of low-income housing should estimate development-related administration costs on the basis of such experience, as applicable, for the current development method. For turnkey projects, there will be less administration activity than for conventional projects. The amounts for the various subaccounts shall be the costs of the items of expense which are directly traceable to and essential in the planning, construction and completion of the project, and the prorata amounts of the PHA's total administration costs with respect to the items which are not wholly traceable to the project. Administration (1410) and Planning (1430) Costs ordinarily terminate with the End of the Initial Operating Period. After this date, only costs of personnel employed full time in development work may be charged to these accounts.

3. 1420 – Interest (lines 22 through 26).
For turnkey projects, because of the limited PHA financing until the completed project is acquired, PHA interest shall be limited to not more than 5 percent for 5 months on the total development cost, excluding interest and contingency. If the project is so planned as to be completed and occupied in several stages, PHA interest shall be computed from the time the PHA takes title to completed increments of the projects to not more than 5 percent for 5 months after completion of the last increment. For a conventional project PP budget, interest shall be limited to not more than 5 percent for each 12 months or portion thereof. For budgets subsequent to the PP Budget, Accounts 1420.1 and .2 shall be charged, to the extent specifically approved by HUD, in accordance with Handbook 7510.1. Line 26, Total Interest, is the amount which results after the deducting interest earned on investments from the interest charged.

4. 1425 – Initial Operating Deficit (line 24).
In the absence of dependable previous experience data on which to base a preliminary estimate of the initial operating deficit, an allowance of not to exceed $50 per dwelling unit may be used unless more is specifically authorized by HUD.

5. 1430 – Planning (lines 25 through 31).
For turnkey projects generally, architectural-engineering services will be included in the Developer's Price except for periodic inspection of construction by an independent architect employed by the PHA (Account 1430.7).

6. 1440.5 – Appraisals (line 36).
No entry shall be made in this Account when HUD performs the appraisal since no fee will be charged. This Account shall be charged with the costs incurred by the PHA for appraisals of land or improvements when provided by fee appraisers.

7. Donations (lines 53 and 54).
Account 2850 is described in Handbook 7510.1. A donation represents cash and/or the reasonable value of property donated to the project. Any costs met from cash donations and the value of any donations in kind will be included under the appropriate cost account and itemized in Subpart VI. Since donations cannot be included in the Total Development Cost, the total of donations will be subtracted therefrom in Subpart I of the Budget.

8. Contingency (line 56).
Enter not more than 5 percent for conventional projects, nor more than 1 percent for turnkey, of the Total Before Contingency.

C. Subpart III – Supporting Data for Cost Estimate in Account 1475 (Lines 6 and 48).
Generally, the PHA provides nondwelling equipment, requiring an entry in line 48 only. Include only nondwelling equipment intended for use in developing the specific project. Account 1475 shall not include automotive passenger vehicles; and shall not, without detailed, itemized justification fully endorsed by the officials involved in its approval, exceed one-half of one percent of the project's Total Development Cost.

D. Subpart IV – New Construction-Prototype Comparison Percentage
The accounts used in this comparison—1460 and 1465 (lines 3, 4, 45 and 46)—should be carefully prepared. It is particularly important that nondwelling construction and equipment costs (chargeable to Accounts 1470 and 1475) not be combined with the dwelling construction and equipment costs in Accounts 1460 and 1465 because this could adversely affect the prototype comparison percentage. Care should also be taken to assure that, in the case of a turnkey project where the developer and the PHA will each provide certain items of dwelling equipment, the amount in Item A2 of this Subpart is the sum of lines 4 and 46.

form **HUD-52484** (8/96)
ref Handbook 7417.1

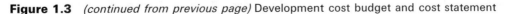

Figure 1.3 *(continued from previous page)* Development cost budget and cost statement

USDA-RD
Form RD 440-11
(Rev.10-00)

ESTIMATE OF FUNDS NEEDED
FOR
30-Day Period Commencing

FORM APPROVED
OMB NO. 0575-0015

Name of Borrower _____

Items	Amount of Funds
Development	$
Contract or Job No. _____	
Contract or Job No. _____	
Contract or Job No. _____	
Land and Rights-of-Way	
Legal Services...	
Engineering Fees	
Interest	
Equipment	
Contingencies	
Refinancing	
Initial O & M	
Other	
TOTAL	$ 0.00

Prepared by _____

By _____
Name of Borrower

Date _____

Approved by _____

Date _____

Position 2

RD 440-11 (Rev. 10-00)

Figure 1.4   Sample of a form to use when estimating the amount of money needed for a project

Position 3

FORM APPROVED
OMB No. 0575-0015

Form RD 442-3
(Rev. 3-97)

Name

BALANCE SHEET

Address

	Month Day Year *Current Year*	Month Day Year *Prior Year*
ASSETS		
CURRENT ASSETS		
1. Cash on hand in Banks		
2. Time deposits and short-term investments		
3. Accounts receiveable		
4. Less: Allowance for doubtful accounts	( )	( )
5. Inventories		
6. Prepayments		
7. _____		
8. _____		
9. Total Current Assets (*Add 1 through 8*)		
FIXED ASSETS		
10. Land		
11. Buildings		
12 Furniture and equipment		
13. _____		
14. Less: Accumulated depreciation	( )	( )
15. Net Total Fixed Assets (*Add 10 through 14*)		
OTHER ASSETS		
16. _____		
17. _____		
18. Total Assets (Add 9, 15, 16 and 17)		
LIABILITIES AND EQUITIES		
CURRENT LIABILITIES		
19. Accounts payable		
20. Notes payable		
21. Current portion of USDA note		
22. Customer deposits		
23. Taxes payable		
24. Interest payable		
25. _____		
26. _____		
27. Total Current Liabilities (*Add 19 through 26*)		
LONG-TERM LIABILITIES		
28. Notes payable USDA		
29. _____		
30. _____		
31. Total Long-Term Liabilities (*Add 28 through 30*)		
32. Total Liabilities (*Add 27 and 31*)		
EQUITY		
33. Retained earnings		
34. Memberships		
35. Total Equity (*Add lines 33 and 34*)		
36. Total Liabilities and Equity (*Add lines 32 and 35*)		

CERTIFIED CORRECT	Date	Appropriate Official *(Signature)*

RD 442-3 (Rev. 3-97)

Figure 1.5 A balance sheet will be needed when applying for development loans, and this is an example of such a form. *(continued on next page)*

INSTRUCTIONS

Present Borrowers

This form may be used as a year end Balance Sheet by Rural Development Community Program and Farm Service Agency Group Farm Loan Program borrowers who do not have an independent audit. Submit two copies within 60 days following year's end to the Agency Official. An independently audited balance sheet will substitute for this form.

Applicants

In preparing this form when the application for financing is for a facility which is a unit of your overall operation, two balance sheets are to be submitted: one for the facility being financed and one for the entire operation. Examples: (a) application to finance a

sewage system which is a part of a water-sewage system or municipality, (b) application to finance a nursing home which is part of a larger health care facility.

Preparation of this Form

1. Enter data where appropriate for the current and prior year.

2. Line 35, Total Equity, of this form will be the same as line 26, on Form RD 442-2, "Statement of Budget, Income and Equity", when using the form.

3. The term Equity is used interchangeably with Net Worth, Fund Balance, etc.

BALANCE SHEET ITEMS

Current Assets

1. Cash on hand and in Banks
   Includes undeposited cash and demand deposits.

2. Time Deposits and Short Term Investments
   Funds in savings accounts and certificates of deposit maturing within one year.

3. Accounts Receivable
   Amounts billed but not paid by customers, users, etc. This is the gross amount before any allowances in item 4.

4. Allowance for Doubtful Accounts
   Amounts included in item 3 which are estimated to be uncollectible.

5. Inventories
   The total of all materials, supplies and finished goods on hand.

6. Prepayments
   Payments made in advance of receipt of goods or utilization of services. Examples: rent, insurance.

7 - 8.   List other current assets not included above.

Fixed Assets

10 - 12.   List land, buildings, furniture and equipment separately by gross value.

13.   List other fixed assets.

14. Accumulated Depreciation
Indicate total accumulated depreciation for items 10-13.

Other Assets

16 - 17.   List other assets not previously accounted for.

Current Liabilities

19. Accounts Payable
    Amounts due to creditors for goods delivered or services completed.

20. Notes Payable
    Amounts due to banks and other creditors for which a promissory note has been signed.

21. Current Portion USDA Note
    Amount due USDA for principal payment during the next 12 months. Includes any payments which are in arrears.

22. Customer Deposits
    Funds of various kinds held for others.

23. Taxes Payable

24. Interest Payable USDA
    Interest applicable to principal amount in line 21.

25 - 26.   List other payables and accruals not shown above.

Long Term Liabilities

28. Notes Payable USDA
    List total principal payments to USDA which mature after one year and are not included in line 21.

29 - 30.   List all other long term liabilities such as bonds, bank loans, etc. which are due after one year.

Equity

33. Retained Earnings
    Net income which has been accumulated from the beginning of the operation and not distributed to members, users, etc.

34. Memberships
    The total of funds collected from persons of membership type facilities, i.e., water and sewer systems.

RD 442-3   Page 2 of 2

Figure 1.5 *(continued from previous page)* A balance sheet will be needed when applying for development loans, and this is an example of such a form.

FORMS MANUAL INSERT   **FORM RD 442-3**

Used by
Rural Development
Community Program
and Farm Service
Agency Group Farm
Loan Program
applicants and
borrowers.

(see reverse)

PROCEDURE FOR PREPARATION   : RD Instructions 1942-A, 1951-E and 1955-A.

PREPARED BY   : Applicant/Borrower.

NUMBER OF COPIES   : Applicant - Original and one copy.
                               Borrower - Original and three copies.

SIGNATURES REQUIRED   : Appropriate Applicant/Borrower Official.

DISTRIBUTION OF COPIES   : Applicant - Original to County case docket; copy retained by
                               Applicant. Borrower - Original and two copies to County; copy
                               retained by Borrower; original to case docket, two copies to State
                               Office (for Community Program delinquent Borrowers, State Office
                               will sent copy to National Office).

Figure 1.5 *(continued from previous page)* A balance sheet will be needed when applying for development loans, and this is an example of such a form.

Form RD 442-2   *Position 3*   FORM APPROVED
(Rev. 9-97)   UNITED STATES DEPARTMENT OF AGRICULTURE   OMB NO. 0575-0015
                                     STATEMENT OF BUDGET, INCOME AND EQUITY

Schedule 1

Name   Address

(1) OPERATING INCOME	PRIOR YEAR Actual (2)	ANNUAL BUDGET BEG _____ END _____ (3)	For the _____ Months Ended _____ CURRENT YEAR		Actual YTD (Over) Under Budget Col. 3 – 5 = 6 (6)
			Actual Data		
			Current Quarter (4)	Year To Date (5)	
1. _____					
2. _____					
3. _____					
4. _____					
5. Miscellaneous					
6. Less: Allowances and Deductions					
7. Total Operating Income (Add lines 1 through 6)					
OPERATING EXPENSES					
8. _____					
9. _____					
10. _____					
11. _____					
12. _____					
13. _____					
14. _____					
15. Interest					
16. Depreciation					
17. Total Operating Expense (Add Lines 8 through 16)					
18. NET OPERATING INCOME (LOSS) (Line 7 less 17)					
NONOPERATING INCOME					
19. _____					
20. _____					
21. Total Nonoperating Income (Add 19 and 20)					
22. NET INCOME (LOSS) (Add lines 18 and 21)					
23. Equity Beginning of Period					
24. _____					
25. _____					
26. Equity End of Period (Add lines 22 through 25)					

Budget and Annual Report Approved by Governing Body   Quarterly Reports Certified Correct

_____   _____   _____   _____
Secretary   Date   Appropriate Official   Date

According to the Paperwork Reduction Act of 1995, no persons are required to respond to a collection of information unless it displays a valid OMB control number. The valid OMB control number for this information collection is 0575-0015. The time required to complete this information collection is estimated to average 2-1/2 hours per response, including the time for reviewing instructions, searching existing data sources, gathering and maintaining the data needed, and completing and reviewing the collection of information.

Figure 1.6 Statement of budget, income, and equity for establishing a financial picture that a lender can consider. *(continued on next page)*

Schedule 1
Page 2

SUPPLEMENTAL DATA

The Following Data Should Be Supplied Where Applicable

1. ALL BORROWERS   Circle One

   a. Are deposited funds in institutions insured by the Federal Government?   Yes   No

   b. Are you exempt from Federal Income Tax?   Yes   No

   c. Are Local, State and Federal Taxes paid current?   Yes   No

   d. Is corporate status in good standing with State?   Yes   No

   e. List kinds and amounts of insurance and fidelity bond: Complete Only when submitting annual budget information:

Insurance Coverage and Policy Number	Insurance Company and Address	Amount of Coverage	Expiration Date of Policy
Property Insurance Policy # _____	_____	_____	_____
Liability Policy # _____	_____	_____	_____
Fidelity Policy # _____	_____	_____	_____

2. RECREATION AND GRAZING ASSOCIATION BORROWERS ONLY   Current Quarter   Year to Date

   a. Number of Members

3. WATER AND/OR SEWER UTILITY BORROWERS ONLY

   a. Water purchased or produced (CU FT - GAL)

   b. Water sold (CU FT - GAL)

   c. Treated waste (CU FT - GAL)

   d. Number of users - water

   e. Number of users - sewer

4. OTHER UTILITIES

   a. Number of users

   b. Product purchased

   c. Product sold

5. HEALTH CARE BORROWERS ONLY

   a. Number of beds

   b. Patient days of care

   c. Percentage of occupancy   %   %

   d. Number of outpatient visits

6. DISTRIBUTION OF ALL CASH AND INVESTMENTS*

   Indicate balances in the following accounts:

	Construction	Revenue	Debt Service	Operation & Maintenance	Reserve	All Others	Grand Total
Cash Savings and Investments	$ _____	$ _____	$ _____	$ _____	$ _____	$ _____	$ _____
	$ _____	$ _____	$ _____	$ _____	$ _____	$ _____	$ _____
Total	$ _____	$ _____	$ _____	$ _____	$ _____	$ _____	$ _____

7. AGE ACCOUNTS RECEIVABLE AS FOLLOWS:

	Days				
	0–30	31–60	61–90	91 and Older	*Total
Dollar Values	$ _____	$ _____	$ _____	$ _____	$ _____
Number of Accounts	_____	_____	_____	_____	_____

*Totals must agree with those on Balance Sheet.

Figure 1.6 *(continued from previous page)* Statement of budget, income, and equity for establishing a financial picture that a lender can consider.

PROJECTED CASH FLOW   Schedule 2

For the Year BEG. _____ END. _____
(same as schedule 1 column 3)

A. Line 22 from Schedule 1, Column 3 NET INCOME (LOSS) .... $ _____

    Add

B. <u>Items in Operations not Requiring Cash:</u>

    1. Depreciation (line 16 schedule 1) .... _____

    2. Others: _____ .... _____

C. <u>Cash Provided From:</u>

    1. Proceeds from Agency loan/grant .... _____

    2. Proceeds from others .... _____

    3. Increase (Decrease) in Accounts Payable, Accruals and other Current Liabilities .... _____

    4. Decrease (Increase) in Accounts Receivable, Inventories and

        Other Current Assets (<u>Exclude cash</u>) .... _____

    5. Other: _____ .... _____

    6. _____ .... _____

D. Total all A, B and C Items .... _____

E. <u>Less:</u> <u>Cash Expended for:</u>

    1. All Construction, Equipment and New Capital Items (loan & grant funds) .... _____

    2. Replacement and Additions to Existing Property, Plant and Equipment .... _____

    3. Principal Payment Agency Loan .... _____

    4. Principal Payment Other Loans .... _____

    5. Other: _____ .... _____

    6. Total E 1 through 5 .... _____

    Add

F. Beginning Cash Balances .... _____

G. Ending Cash Balances (Total of D Minus E 6 Plus F) .... $ _____

<u>Item G Cash Balances Composed of:</u>

Construction Account .... $ _____

Revenue Account .... _____

Debt Payment Account .... _____

O&M Account .... _____

Reserve Account .... _____

Funded Depreciation Account .... _____

Others: _____ .... _____

_____ .... _____

Total - Agrees with Item G .... $ _____

Figure 1.6 *(continued from previous page)* Statement of budget, income, and equity for establishing a financial picture that a lender can consider.

STATEMENT OF BUDGET, INCOME AND EQUITY
INSTRUCTIONS

Community Program Borrowers

Frequency and Preparation:

1.   When used as Management Report.
    (a)   Prior to the beginning of each fiscal year, complete only column three, "Annual Budget," for the next fiscal year on page 1 and forward two copies to the County Supervisor. All data should be entered on the same basis as your accounting records, i.e., cash, accrual, etc. The budget must be approved by the governing body. Schedule 2, Projected Cash Flow will also be prepared and submitted at the same time.

    (b)   Twenty (20) days after the end of each of the 1st 3 quarters of each year, complete all data on pages one and two and forward two copies to the County Supervisor. For 4th quarter Management Report, see (2) and (3) below.

2.   When used as a year end Statement of Income. For borrowers not required to have an independent audit, and who are required to furnish Management Reports, complete all information on both pages of Schedule 1. This will serve as the 4th quarter Management Report and year end financial Statement of Income. This Annual Report will be approved by the governing body, with two copies submitted within 60 days of year end to the County Supervisor.

    For borrowers who are not required to furnish Management Reports, page 1 of schedule 1 may be used for the Annual Statement of Income if an annual audit is not required. In this case, complete only columns 1, 2 and 5.

Note: Year End Balance Sheet is also required in either of the aforementioned situations.

3.   An independently audited Statement of Income containing budget and actual data will substitute for page 1 of this form as the 4th quarter Management Report, when required, and the year end Statement of Income. However, page 2 must be completed for all borrowers required to submit Management Reports.

Group Farmer Program Borrowers   1949-B (442.9)

Frequency and Preparation:

1.   When used as Management Report submit Budget Data Only. Complete column three, "Annual Budget," for the next fiscal year on page 1, Schedule 1 and forward two copies to the County Supervisor. All data should be entered on the same basis as your accounting records, i.e., cash, accrual, etc. The budget must be approved by the governing body. When submitting along with Statement of Income, (item 2 below) include this budget data at the same time. Schedule 2, Projected Cash Flow is not required.

2.   When used as year end Statement of Income. For borrowers not required to have independent audits, page 1 of Schedule 1 may be used for the Annual Statement of Income. Complete columns 1, 2 and 5. Also complete items 1, 6 and 7 on page 2. This form must be approved by the governing body, with two copies submitted within 60 days of year end to the County Supervisor. An independently audited Statement of Income will substitute for page 1, Schedule 1.

Column and Line Item Preparation

Column 1
Income and Expense Items:
All data entered should be on the same basis as your Accounting Record, i.e., Cash Basis, Accrual Basis, etc.

Operating Income
Lines 1 – 5   List types of income as appropriate.
Line 6   Allowances and Deductions
                   (Pertains Generally to Health Care Institutions, and represents the difference between Gross Income and Amounts Received or to be Received from Patient and third party payors)

Operating Expenses
Lines 8 – 14   List types of expenses as appropriate
Line 15   Interest Agency
                   (Interest expense incurred on Agency note(s).)
Line 16   Depreciation
                   (Total depreciation expense for the year)
Line 18   Net Operating Income (Loss)
                   (This amount represents the net operating income or loss before adding income not related to operations below)

Figure 1.6 *(continued from previous page)* Statement of budget, income, and equity for establishing a financial picture that a lender can consider.

INSTRUCTIONS - Column and Line Item Preparation Cont'd

<u>Non Operating Income</u>
Line 19 – 20	(Indicate items of income derived from sources other than regular activities, EX: interest, earned)
Line 22	<u>Net Income (Loss)</u>

(This amount is also transferred to item A of the Projected Cash Flow statement Schedule 2 when Management Reports are required for Community Program borrowers only.

Line 23	<u>Equity, Beginning of Period</u>

(Enter the Equity at the beginning of Reporting Period. The term Equity is used interchangeably with Net Worth and Fund Balance.)

Lines 24 – 25   Enter items which cause changes in the Current Year's Equity other than line 22 amount.

Lines 26   <u>Equity End of Period</u>

(This balance will be the same amount that appears on the Balance Sheet.)

Column 2 -   <u>Prior Year Actual</u>

Enter the actual income, expense and equity amounts of the prior year.

<u>Community Program Borrowers:</u> Use this column for all management report requirements except when submitting the proposed budget prior to the beginning of each fiscal year. Also fill in when using this Schedule as the year-end Statement of Income.

<u>Group Farmer Programs:</u> Complete only when also using this form as annual Statement of Income.

Column 3 -   <u>Annual Budget</u>

This will be the budget for the <u>current year</u> when actual data is presented in columns four and/or five. When submitting <u>only</u> budget data on this form, the amounts will be for the next year. Enter the beginning and ending dates of the budget year at the top of this column.

Column 4 -   <u>Actual Data, Current Quarter</u>

Only used by Community Program borrowers required to submit Management Reports and contains information for the current three months being reported.

Column 5 -   <u>Actual Data, Year to Date</u>

For borrowers submitting Management Reports, enter cumulative data from the beginning of the Accounting Year through the Current Quarter. When used as Fourth Quarter Management Report and/or year end Statement of Income, enter data for the entire year.

Column 6 -   <u>Actual Year to Date (over) Under Budget</u>

Only used by borrowers required to submit Management Reports and is determined by subtracting column 5 from column 3 for each line item.

     <u>SCHEDULE 1, PAGE 2, SUPPLEMENTAL DATA</u>

This information is required of all borrowers submitting Management Reports. Fill in as indicated.

<u>Community Program</u> Borrowers complete as appropriate.

<u>Group Farmer Program</u> Borrowers complete only items 1, 6 and 7.

Figure 1.6 *(continued from previous page)* Statement of budget, income, and equity for establishing a financial picture that a lender can consider.

PROJECTED CASH FLOW
INSTRUCTIONS

The completion of this form is required of all Community Program borrowers submitting Management Reports, and will accompany Schedule 1 when the Annual Budget is transmitted, to the County Supervisor. See Instruction No. 1 on Schedule 1.

This form is used to Project the Flow of cash for the budget year in order to determine the adequacy of cash to cover Operating Expenses, Transfer to Reserves, Debt Payment, Capital Outlays, etc.

Cash Basis Account - Systems

Borrowers who maintain their records strictly on the cash basis of accounting and have no Accounts Receivable and Accounts Payable, will probably only need to complete the following line items:
A, B-1, C-1, E-1 and E-3, F and G.

Line Item Instructions

Line A - Bring forward the income or loss as entered on line 22, schedule 1, column 3.

Line B - Add back any depreciation or other non cash items included on schedule 1, column 3.

Line C - Complete items C-1 through C-6 as appropriate, for item changes which provide for increase in cash balances.
    Note: Do not include changes in Cash Accounts, in Current Assets of item C-4. Lines C-3 and C-4 will indicate the changes in Working Capital (Current Assets and Current Liabilities, Exclusive of Cash.)

Line D - Enter the net total of all A, B and C items.

Line E - Complete items E-1 through E-6 as appropriate for items for which cash was expended.

Line F - Enter the Beginning Cash Balance(s) for the Period.

Line G - The total of item D less E-6 plus F will be the Ending Cash Balance(s). This total will be reconciled by balances in the Various Accounts, i.e., Construction, Revenue, Debt, etc.

Figure 1.6 *(continued from previous page)* Statement of budget, income, and equity for establishing a financial picture that a lender can consider.

Your Company Name
Your Company Address
Your Company Phone and Fax Numbers

BUSINESS CREDIT APPLICATION

Please supply ALL required information. Only FULLY COMPLETED forms will be considered.

Company name: _____

Trade name: _____

Billing address: _____

Headquarters address: _____

Telephone: _____ Fax: _____ Telex: _____

Subsidiary of _____ Address: _____

____ Corporation ____ Partnership ____ Proprietor ____ Other: _____

Year established: _____ Type of business: _____

Yearly sales: $_____ Yearly profits: $_____ Net Worth: $_____

Resale tax #: _____ Tax exemption #: _____ Employer ID#: _____

Please list partners (partnership), owner (proprietorship), officers (all others):

Name: _____ Title: _____ Soc. Sec. #_____

Address: _____

Name: _____ Title: _____ Soc. Sec. #_____

Address: _____

Name: _____ Title: _____ Soc. Sec. #_____

Address: _____

Applicant agrees the following apply to all purchases and credit, if allowed:

1. All overdue invoices bear interest at _____ (____%) percent per month on unpaid balance.
2. Processing charge of $_____ for each chargeback of unearned discounts.
3. Applicant will pay all costs of collection, including but not limited to attorney fees and court costs.
4. Credit line may be terminated, altered, suspended, or otherwise changed at any time, with or without cause, by Vendor.
5. The terms of all transactions shall be as stated on Vendor's documents, which shall govern all transactions, regardless of conflicts, if any, with Applicant's documentation.
6. All transactions shall be governed by the laws of Vendor's jurisdiction.

Page 1 of 2.

Figure 1.7 Whether you are extending credit or applying for credit, a credit application will be needed, and this is an example of such an application. *(continued on next page)*

Business Credit Application (continued)   Page 2 of 2.

Bank References

Bank name: _____   Account number: _____

Address: _____   Telephone number: _____

Bank name: _____   Account number: _____

Address: _____   Telephone number: _____

Trade Credit References

Vendor name: _____   Account number: _____

Address: _____   Telephone number: _____

Vendor name: _____   Account number: _____

Address: _____   Telephone number: _____

Other Credit References

Creditor: _____   Account number: _____

Address: _____   Telephone number: _____

Creditor: _____   Account number: _____

Address: _____   Telephone number: _____

Please attach most recent balance sheet and profit and loss statement or income tax return. (Credit cannot be allowed without financial statements and references.)

All information provided in connection with this Business Credit Application, including all financial statements, tax returns, and other materials, if any, is true, complete, and correct. Applicant agrees to update and supplement this information on demand, and further agrees to notify Vendor immediately in the event of any change in circumstances that might reasonably affect Vendor's ability to collect from Applicant, or Vendor's willingness to extend credit, or both. Applicant hereby authorizes Vendor to contact all references, whether listed herein or not, and to receive therefrom all credit information, including confidential information, as Vendor may request. Applicant understands acceptance of this Application by Vendor does not constitute an extension of credit nor a promise to extend credit. Any extension of credit by Vendor does not constitute a promise to extend additional or future credit.

_____   _____   _____
Date   Applicant's signature   Title

Figure 1.7   *(continued from previous page)* Whether you are extending credit or applying for credit, a credit application will be needed, and this is an example of such an application.

Chapter 2

Putting Your Plans Together

Land development is a field of work that requires a lot of planning. There are different types of planning. You have to plan a budget, a development strategy, a marketing plan, and so forth. There is no easy answer. You have to do the work, but it's worth it. It is not uncommon for land developers to double their money on a deal.

This chapter focuses on the types of plans that you will have to submit to local authorities for approval. These are the plans that make a project move forward. The other planning is equally important. You can't take any planning for granted. The intent here is to identify the types of plan submissions that you will need to get the ball rolling.

Subdivision Regulations to Consider				
Topic	Considered	Acceptable	Unacceptable	Need More Data
Zoning				
Easements				
Deed restrictions				
Covenants				
Road access				
Public sewer				
Public water main				
Public gas main				
Tap fees for connecting to public utilities				
Street design				
Walkways				
Signage				
Green space requirements				
Erosion protection				
Environmental regulations				
Building restrictions				
Minimum lot-size requirements				

Checklist 2.1   Subdivision regulations to consider

Components of Construction Plans for Land Development				
Component	**Have**	**Need**	**Don't Need**	**Ordered**
Cover sheet				
Site conditions				
Vicinity map				
Symbol legends				
Developer's name				
Development name				
Grading plan				
Site plan				
Existing buildings plan				
Proposed buildings plan				
Road plans				
Utility plans				
Parking areas				
Storm water drawings				
Existing contours				
Proposed contours				
Sediment and erosion plan				
Landscaping plan				
Easement details				

Checklist 2.2 Components of construction plans for land development

Components of Final Project Development Plans

Component	Included	Not Yet Included	Not Needed
Project name			
Project section (for large developments)			
Surveys			
Legal description of property			
Names of property owners			
Right-of-ways			
Easements			
Names of streets			
Lot addresses			
Covenants			
Restrictions			
Building plans			
Restricted areas			

Checklist 2.3 Components of final project development plans

Agency Approvals That May Be Needed			
Agency	**Need**	**Don't Need**	**Have**
Zoning department			
Environmental Protection Agency			
Department of Environmental Protection			
Soil conservation district			
Public works department			
Department of education			
Fire and rescue department			
Building codes enforcement			
Parks and recreation department			
Local specific utility agencies			

Checklist 2.4   Agency approvals that may be needed

Components for a Project Design				
Component	**Need**	**Don't Need**	**Need More Data**	**Have**
Project drawings				
Site plan				
Elevation plan				
Surveys				
Overview plan				
Zoning maps				
Topographical maps				
Transportation drawings				
Utility plans and maps				
Road designs				
Proposed lot sizes and locations				
Landscaping plan				
Housing plan				
Recreational area plans				
Greenspace plans				
Common area plans				
Waterways and pond plans				

Checklist 2.5   Components for a project design

Components of a Preliminary Plan				
Component	Checked	Approved	Not Approved	Not Applicable
Soils test				
Geology reports				
Zoning requirements				
Site plan				
Defined land use				
Street design				
Traffic signage				
Utility plan				
Easement verifications				
Wastewater plan				
Lot sizes and locations				

Checklist 2.6 Components of a preliminary plan

PLAN NAME:_____ EFFECTIVE: August 8, 1994

CHECKLIST FOR MINOR SITE PLANS

Minor site plan can only be submitted if this form has been signed by authorized Planning Personnel.

All Minor Site Plan Applications must include the following information:

CEM CODE	Yes	No	N/A
FO 1. All property lines and the centerline of the State Road along the front of the site.			
FO 2. The entrance (curb cut) location including the distance to the nearest street intersection and sight distance.			
FO 3. Travelways (aisles) and parking spaces. Show dimensions. (The DCSM requires a dustless surface.)			
FO 4. All existing and proposed buildings to scale and labeled "existing" or "proposed."			
FO 5. Distances from the property line to the existing and proposed structures (front, back and side yards.)			
FO 6. Building height.			
FO 7. Any fences, noting the type of fence.			
FO 8. Any outside storage areas, including refuse removal. (Screening is required.)			
FO 9. Proposed sanitary and water facilities.			
FO 10. A letter of request for waiver of any of the above requirements must be submitted to the Director of the Office of Planning.			
FO 11. A letter explaining the intended use of the property should be submitted with the plan.			

_____   _____
Engineer/Surveyor Signature   Date

_____   _____
Office of Planning Authorized   Date

Checklist 2.7   Checklist for minor site plans

Effective: February 18, 1997

PRINCE WILLIAM COUNTY OFFICE OF PLANNING

PLAN NAME: _____

MINIMUM SUBMISSION REQUIREMENTS FOR FINAL PLATS
(Simple, Family Subdivision, Resubdivision, Consolidation, Rights-of-Way Dedication
Easement, Abandonment, Vacation and Revision to Approved Plats)

CEM CODE	ADMINISTRATIVE ITEMS	Admin. Procedures Section	YES	NO	N/A
D01	Fees in accordance with the Fee Schedule. A certified Prince William County (PWC) Review Fee Calculation Sheet.	4.05.1			
D02	Standard Prince William County Development Control Form with all required information. (If not signed by the owner, a Power of Attorney must accompany this form.)	4.05.2(A1)			
D03	Existing zoning of parcel.				
D04	Reference to rezoning file, if applicable.				
	PLAT DETAILS				
D05	Sheet size and lettering in accordance with Va. State Library Board.	4.05.5(B1)			
D06	Graphic scale of lot less than 1" = 100' (metric ratio 1:1,000).	4.05.5(B2)			
D07	Title block, including subdivision name or owner's name, engineer's/surveyor's name and address, magisterial district, date, description of plat and project number. The project number is assigned by Information Resources prior to submission.	4.05.5(B3)			
D08	North arrow and designation of north orientation used for survey. Appropriate note provided for plats referencing VCS 1983.	4.05.5(B4a,b, c)			
D09	Complete VCS coordinates for two corners on each sheet, if applicable.	4.05.5(B5)			
D10	Vicinity map (scale 1" = 2000') (metric ratio 1:25,000).	4.05.5(B6)			
D11	Seal (on each sheet) by a Virginia registered engineer or land surveyor. Seals are not required to be signed until approval submission, provided the following note is added: "This plat is for review purposes only and not for recordation."	4.05.5(B7)			
D12	Surveyor's/engineer's certificate.	4.05.5(B7)			
D13	Owner's consent and dedication (owner's notarized signature prior to approval submission).	4.05.5(B9a)			
D14	Area of each lot or parcel shown less than 10 acres (4.05 hectares) in size and included in area tabulation (indicate residue for parcels greater than 10 acres (4.05 hectares)).	4.05.5(B10)			
D15	Area tabulation indicating total site area, number of lots, residue area, etc.	4.05.5(B11)			
D16	Individual lots each identified by a separate and sequential number in accordance with Section 603.24 of the DCSM.	4.05.5(B12)			
D17	Existing parcel's GPINs and all adjacent parcels' GPINs or GSINs.	4.05.5(B13)			
D18	Subdivision, parcel and lot boundaries with bearings, distances and complete curve table. (Curve data must be on same sheet as the curve it describes.)	4.05.5(B14)			
D19	All existing structures shown on the plat or an exhibit for resubdivisions, consolidations, and family subdivisions.	4.05.5(15)			
D20	All applicable notes.	4.05.5(B16)			
D21	Addresses shown for existing lots in accordance with Section 603.24 of the DCSM. (New addresses will be assigned during the reivew process as necessary.)	4.05.3(B17)			
D22	100-year flood area boundaries, including ties to property lines and corners with bearings, distances and/or curve data, and labeled "Flood Hazard Area."	4.05.5(B18)			
D23	The RPA boundary, when applicable, including ties to property lines and corners, with bearings, distances and/or curve data.	4.05.5(B19)			
D24	The RMA boundary, when applicable, including ties to property lines and corners, with bearings, distances and/or curve data.	4.05.5(B20)			

Figure 2.1 Minimum submission requirements for final plats *(continued on next page)*

D25	Existing and proposed easements, types, widths, bearings, distances, and/or curve data for centerlines. Deed book and page references for existing easements and appropriate maintenance note for all proposed easements, such as sight distance, utility, buffer, storm drainage, water, sanitary sewer, etc.	4.05.5(B21)			
D26	Existing and proposed street right-of-way boundaries within, adjacent to, or providing access to the site with bearings, distances, and/or curve data, centerline, street name, route number or deed book and page number. New right-of-way dedication with the following phrase, "Hereby Dedicated for Public Street Purposes."	4.05.5(B22)			
D27	Vacated street or parcels showing areas vacated and area amounts reverted to adjacent parcels.	4.05.5(B23)			
D28	Existing and proposed drainfield locations shown on the plat or an exhibit, and the following note (if applicable) added to the plat. "the proposed drainfield(s) shall provide a reserve drainfield area at least equal to that of the primary sewage disposal site."	4.05.5(B24)			
D29	Existing and proposed well locations shown on the plat or an exhibit.	4.05.5(B25)			
D30	Application for a family subdivision including the deed by which the owner obtained the property, deed transferring the property, and proof of relationship.	4.05.5(26)			
D31	All existing easements, with deed book and page number, or a note stating that "All underlying easements may not be indicated on this plat."	4.05.5(B27)			
D32	The following note shall be included on the plat for all site or subdivision plats that include a landscape plan. "The owner of fee title to any property on which plant material has been established in accordance with an approved landscape/planting plan shall be responsible for the maintenance, repair and replacement of the approved plant material as required by the ordinance." (If a plat is not required, the note above shall be shown on the landscape or grading plan.)	4.05.5(B28)			
D33	Every use requiring establishment of a buffer area shall note the following restriction regarding the use of such buffer on a plat or other instrument recorded among the land records: "Land designated as buffer area shall be landscaped and may only be used for structures, uses, or facilities in accordance with the requirements of the Zoning Ordinance and the DCSM."	4.05.5(B29)			

I HEREBY CERTIFY THAT THE STATED INFORMATION IS INCLUDED IN THE ATTACHED PLAN AND/OR DOCUMENTS.

DATE:_____   _____
                                              Engineer/Surveyor Signature

ce:land:chklist4

Figure 2.1   *(continued from previous page)* Minimum submission requirements for final plats

Effective: February 18, 1997

PRINCE WILLIAM COUNTY OFFICE OF PLANNING

PLAN NAME: _____

MINIMUM SUBMISSION REQUIREMENTS FOR FINAL PLATS
(Simple, Family Subdivision, Resubdivision, Consolidation, Rights-of-Way Dedication
Easement, Abandonment, Vacation and Revision to Approved Plats)

CEM CODE	ADMINISTRATIVE ITEMS	Admin. Procedures Section	YES	NO	N/A
D01	Fees in accordance with the Fee Schedule. A certified Prince William County (PWC) Review Fee Calculation Sheet.	4.05.1			
D02	Standard Prince William County Development Control Form with all required information. (If not signed by the owner, a Power of Attorney must accompany this form.)	4.05.2(A1)			
D03	Existing zoning of parcel.				
D04	Reference to rezoning file, if applicable.				
	PLAT DETAILS				
D05	Sheet size and lettering in accordance with Va. State Library Board.	4.05.5(B1)			
D06	Graphic scale of lot less than 1" = 100' (metric ratio 1:1,000).	4.05.5(B2)			
D07	Title block, including subdivision name or owner's name, engineer's/surveyor's name and address, magisterial district, date, description of plat and project number. The project number is assigned by Information Resources prior to submission.	4.05.5(B3)			
D08	North arrow and designation of north orientation used for survey. Appropriate note provided for plats referencing VCS 1983.	4.05.5(B4a,b,c)			
D09	Complete VCS coordinates for two corners on each sheet, if applicable.	4.05.5(B5)			
D10	Vicinity map (scale 1" = 2000') (metric ratio 1:25,000).	4.05.5(B6)			
D11	Seal (on each sheet) by a Virginia registered engineer or land surveyor. Seals are not required to be signed until approval submission, provided the following note is added: "This plat is for review purposes only and not for recordation."	4.05.5(B7)			
D12	Surveyor's/engineer's certificate.	4.05.5(B7)			
D13	Owner's consent and dedication (owner's notarized signature prior to approval submission).	4.05.5(B9a)			
D14	Area of each lot or parcel shown less than 10 acres (4.05 hectares) in size and included in area tabulation (indicate residue for parcels greater than 10 acres (4.05 hectares)).	4.05.5(B10)			
D15	Area tabulation indicating total site area, number of lots, residue area, etc.	4.05.5(B11)			
D16	Individual lots each identified by a separate and sequential number in accordance with Section 603.24 of the DCSM.	4.05.5(B12)			
D17	Existing parcel's GPINs and all adjacent parcels' GPINs or GSINs.	4.05.5(B13)			
D18	Subdivision, parcel and lot boundaries with bearings, distances and complete curve table. (Curve data must be on same sheet as the curve it describes.)	4.05.5(B14)			
D19	All existing structures shown on the plat or an exhibit for resubdivisions, consolidations, and family subdivisions.	4.05.5(15)			
D20	All applicable notes.	4.05.5(B16)			
D21	Addresses shown for existing lots in accordance with Section 603.24 of the DCSM. (New addresses will be assigned during the reivew process as necessary.)	4.05.3(B17)			
D22	100-year flood area boundaries, including ties to property lines and corners with bearings, distances and/or curve data, and labeled "Flood Hazard Area."	4.05.5(B18)			
D23	The RPA boundary, when applicable, including ties to property lines and corners, with bearings, distances and/or curve data.	4.05.5(B19)			
D24	The RMA boundary, when applicable, including ties to property lines and corners, with bearings, distances and/or curve data.	4.05.5(B20)			

Checklist 2.8 Minimum submission requirements checklist *(continued on next page)*

D25	Existing and proposed easements, types, widths, bearings, distances, and/or curve data for centerlines. Deed book and page references for existing easements and appropriate maintenance note for all proposed easements, such as sight distance, utility, buffer, storm drainage, water, sanitary sewer, etc.	4.05.5(B21)			
D26	Existing and proposed street right-of-way boundaries within, adjacent to, or providing access to the site with bearings, distances, and/or curve data, centerline, street name, route number or deed book and page number. New right-of-way dedication with the following phrase, "Hereby Dedicated for Public Street Purposes."	4.05.5(B22)			
D27	Vacated street or parcels showing areas vacated and area amounts reverted to adjacent parcels.	4.05.5(B23)			
D28	Existing and proposed drainfield locations shown on the plat or an exhibit, and the following note (if applicable) added to the plat. "the proposed drainfield(s) shall provide a reserve drainfield area at least equal to that of the primary sewage disposal site."	4.05.5(B24)			
D29	Existing and proposed well locations shown on the plat or an exhibit.	4.05.5(B25)			
D30	Application for a family subdivision including the deed by which the owner obtained the property, deed transferring the property, and proof of relationship.	4.05.5(26)			
D31	All existing easements, with deed book and page number, or a note stating that "All underlying easements may not be indicated on this plat."	4.05.5(B27)			
D32	The following note shall be included on the plat for all site or subdivision plats that include a landscape plan. "The owner of fee title to any property on which plant material has been established in accordance with an approved landscape/planting plan shall be responsible for the maintenance, repair and replacement of the approved plant material as required by the ordinance." (If a plat is not required, the note above shall be shown on the landscape or grading plan.)	4.05.5(B28)			
D33	Every use requiring establishment of a buffer area shall note the following restriction regarding the use of such buffer on a plat or other instrument recorded among the land records: "Land designated as buffer area shall be landscaped and may only be used for structures, uses, or facilities in accordance with the requirements of the Zoning Ordinance and the DCSM."	4.05.5(B29)			

I HEREBY CERTIFY THAT THE STATED INFORMATION IS INCLUDED IN THE ATTACHED PLAN AND/OR DOCUMENTS.

DATE:_____   _____
                                                        Engineer/Surveyor Signature

ce:land:chklist4

Checklist 2.8   *(continued from previous page)* Minimum submission requirements checklist

COUNTY OF PRINCE WILLIAM
1 County Complex Court, Prince William, Virginia 22192-9201
(703) 792-6830   Metro 631-1703, Ext. 6830 FAX (703) 792-4758
Internet   www.pwcgov.org

PLANNING
OFFICE

PROVISIONAL USE APPLICATION PACKET

Enclosed you will find the forms and instructions necessary to file an application for a PUP. All applications must be filed with the appropriate filing fee as indicated on Page 7 & 8 of this packet.

Please provide all information requested. This information will assist the Zoning Office in accurately assessing your proposal, including its consistency with the Prince William County Zoning Ordinance. If a sketch or minor site plan is currently required for the particular use involved, it may be submitted with the initial application. The requirements for sketch plans and minor site plans are found in Section 4.0 of the Administrative Procedures in the Design and Construction Standards Manual (DCSM). Copies of the manuals are available for review in the Office of Planning, Prince William County Libraries, and the Planning Office web page @ http://www.pwcgov.org/planning/

Prior to submitting your application, please contact the Zoning Office to arrange for a pre-application meeting. Applications can not be accepted without a pre-application meeting. This meeting is to be held to review the particulars of the provisional use prior to application; there is no charge for this meeting. Pre-application meetings are important to assure that applications are complete, that all issues are identified, and to assure efficient, timely processing. Please note that additional information may be required, if deemed necessary by the case manager, on the basis of the nature of the provisional use and its proposed location.

Please refer to Page 2 to find a generalized flow chart of the PUP review process. Should you have any questions, please contact the Zoning Office @ (703) 792-6830.

Attachment: PUP application packet

Figure 2.2   Sample provisional use application package *(continued on next page)*

PROVISIONAL USE PERMIT APPLICATION PACKET

Table of Contents

Figure 2.2   *(continued from previous page)* Sample provisional use application package

Answers to frequently asked questions

Q. What is a provisional use?
A. It is a use which by its nature may have impacts on surrounding property, public facilities or other community facilities; usually different in scale or size from uses permitted by right.

Q. What is a provisional use permit?
A. It is a permit which allows provisional uses to be located within designated districts under the controls, limitations, and regulations of the provisional use permit established by Section 32-230.01 of the Zoning Ordinance.

Q. How can a person apply for a provisional use permit?
A. Refer to "Overview of the provisional use permit application process" outlined in the application package.

Q. Who can make an application for a provisional use permit?
A. Any property owner, and any lessee, contract purchaser, official department, board or bureau of any goverment or its agent.

Q. What are the minimum submission requirements for a provisional use permit?
A. Refer to "minimum submission requirements" outlined in the application package.

Q. How long will it take to approve or deny an application for a provisional use permit?
A. The application will be approved or denied within forty-five (45) working days from the initial acceptance of the application.

Q. What will happen if the Zoning Administrator does not approve or deny the application within forty-five (45) calendar days of initial acceptance of the application?
A. Failure by the Zoning Administrator to act within the time period provided may, at the applicant's option, be deemed approved.

Q. What can I do if the application for a provisional use permit is denied?
A. Refer to "overview of the provisional use permit application process" outlined in the application package.

Q. When does a provisional use permit expire?
A. There is no expiration time, however a provisional use permit shall be revocable on the order of the Zoning Administrator at any time because of the owner or operator of the use covered by the permit to observe all requirements of law with respect to the maintenance and conduct of the use and all conditions imposed in connection with the permit.

Figure 2.2 *(continued from previous page)* Sample provisional use application package

PROVISIONAL USE PERMIT
GENERALIZED FLOW CHART(1b)

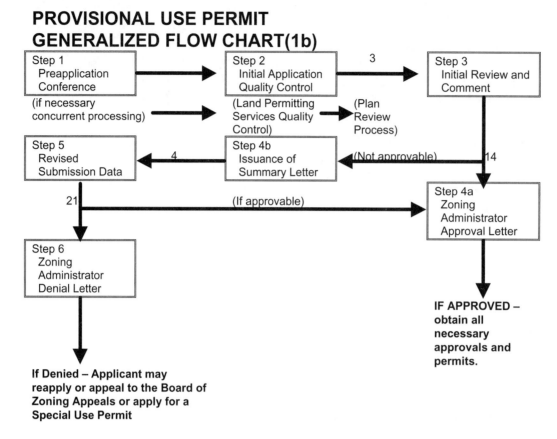

NOTES:
(1) The number between each box represents the estimated number of calendar days to perform the indicated tasks set forth in Part 1 (Maximum total time = 45 days).
(2) Requests for waivers and concurrent processing associated with the Provisional Use Permit application must be submitted to the case manager with the initial submission of an application. During Step 2, a quality review of the application is undertaken. Once the application is found to be "complete," the 45-day mandate for final action commences and the request is considered officially filed.
(3) In Step 4a, approval of the Provisional Use Permit may involve site plan revision, occupancy permits, etc. Contact the Division of Land Permitting Services at 703.792.6830 or Metro 631.1703, ext. 6830 for more details.

Figure 2.2 *(continued from previous page)* Sample provisional use application package

Overview of the provisional use permit application process

STEP 1: Pre-application conference

Prior to submitting an application for a provisional use permit, you must contact the Zoning Office (703-792-6830), and schedule a pre-application conference with the provisional use permit coordinator. The purpose of the meeting is to go over the provisional use permit review process in order to identify the applicable submission requirements and relevant regulations for that particular use. This meeting is held prior to the submission of any materials or the submission of any fees.

If a site plan is required for the commencement of your provisional use permit, the plan may be submitted simultaneously with your application after the submission and approval of a "Request for concurrent processing" (form is available from Zoning Office). The details required for this sketch or minor site plan will be established during the pre-application conference.

STEP 2: Initial application submission/quality control

The completed application is submitted to the Zoning Office. Upon receipt of the application, the Zoning Office will review the application to ensure the items described in the checklist have been included and are complete. If the application is found to be lacking any of the required information, or if the information is deemed to be inaccurate, the application will not be accepted for further processing until all deficiencies have been corrected by you.

If required, the site plan may be submitted at this time. This item is to be in accordance with the requirements of Section 1000.00 of the Design and Construction Standards Manual.

Upon acceptance of the application, a Case Manager will be formally assigned. You will receive written notification of any deficiencies in the application from the Case Manager during the initial review.

Minimum submission requirements - in general

Each provisional use permit (PUP) application must be accompanied by a series of diagrams demonstrating compliance with the various PUP requirements. In addition, a written description of the proposed use is also required. Any information you consider helpful in determining the consistency of your proposal with the relevant regulations should be provided at the outset of the application process. This will help to expedite your application through the review process.

Figure 2.2 *(continued from previous page)* Sample provisional use application package

All provisional use applications must include the following information;

1. Completed standard application form (1copy), refer to page 12 of this packet.

2. Check for fees, payment of fees is required with every application. Refer to page 7&8 of this packet for a current fee schedule.

3. Latest deed or lease agreement. (1 copy)

4. *Accurate plat/vicinity map, (1 copy) an accurate survey plat of the property prepared by a certified land surveyor or licensed civil engineer is required with every application.

The survey plat should contain the following:

❖ Bearings and distances for all property lines and existing zoning district lines

❖ Area of land proposed for consideration, in square feet or acres

❖ Scale and north point

❖ Names of all surrounding roads or streets and widths of existing rights-of-way (including route number)

❖ Parcel identification numbers, present zoning, and land use of all abutting and contiguous parcels, the street address of building or tenant space.

❖ All easements or encumbrances on the property, including lease agreements

❖ All structures, buffers, fences and other similar features on the property must be shown. All setback requirements of the underlying zoning district must be met, regardless of whether associated with provisional use operation or not.

5. **Parking tabulation, showing required and provided parking spaces for the entire site, based upon current uses and demonstrating where the required spaces for the provisional use are available (to be established at pre-application conference by the Case Manager

6. Scale drawing of tenant space or building layout (1 copy), diagram showing gross and/or net floor area (net floor area = 75% of gross floor area), internal partitions, mezzanines, uses for each separated portion, and other details of space. Commercially zoned sites only, not required for home employment uses.

Figure 2.2 *(continued from previous page)* Sample provisional use application package

7. Occupancy load certification from Fire Marshall's Office (if necessary), this depends upon the provisional use and will be determined at the pre-application conference.

8. Hours of operation proposed-if appropriate

9. Estimated number of patrons, clients, etc. – if appropriate

10. Estimated traffic distribution generated, by mode and time of day (this will also be determined at pre-application conference)

Additional information requirements:

Any further information or documentation may be required by the Case Manager to demonstrate compliance with the provisions of this part, based upon the nature or location of the requested provisional use (see Zoning Ordinance section32-230.04(8)). Questions of appropriateness or when given provision, must be completed and are to be resolved during the pre-application meeting. This would include appropriateness of items such as Fire Marshall (occupancy limits) or Police Department (security plan) approvals prior to Certificate of Occupancy, or the initiation of operations.

Waivers:

Except for the filing fee, the Zoning Administrator may waive the submission requirements, or any portion thereof, provided such information is not necessary for the proper review of the application (see Zoning Ordinance section 32-230.04(9)).

A request for such a waiver(s) shall be submitted with the application, with a reason for the request clearly stated. All waiver determinations are to be made within fourteen (14) business days of receipt by the Planning Office.

Initial review and comment

The Case Manager will perform a substantive analysis of the application, and any waiver determinations. The text of the application will be transmitted to the Planning Commission and Board member(s) of the affected magisterial district(s).

If any inconsistencies and/or conflicts are found, the Case Manager will prepare a summary letter specifically identifying any inconsistencies with the provisional use permit requirements or other County regulations. You will be notified of these preliminary findings.

Figure 2.2 *(continued from previous page)* Sample provisional use application package

Summary letter

If the application is found to be inconsistent with the Zoning Ordinance requirements, you may wish to amend your application as outlined in the summary letter from the Case Manager, and return the required documents and information to this office for further consideration.

Revised submission data

The revised submission data and any required documents and/or information will be reviews by the Case Manager. If your proposal is found to be consistent with the Zoning Ordinance, the review of the application will continue.

Approval letter

If your proposal is found to be consistent, you will be called to come into the office to sign the approval letter. The Zoning Administrator will then sign the approval letter, and a copy shall be returned to you for your records. A copy of the approval letter, once signed by the applicant and the Zoning Administrator will be forwarded to the Chairman of the Board of County Supervisors, the Supervisor(s) in whose district(s) the use lies, and any relevant review agencies.

Once the application is approved, the applicant must proceed to obtain any other permits that are shown in the approval letter.

Please note that the approval however, may be appealed by any aggrieved party pursuant to Section 32-900.00 et seq. of the Zoning Ordinance for up to 30 days after the decision of the Zoning Administrator.

Denial letter

If the application is denied, the applicant has two options for recourse.

1. Appeal the determination to the Board of Zoning Appeals pursuant to section 32-900.00 et seq. of the Zoning Ordinance

2. Apply for a Special Use permit in accordance with section 32-700.00 of the Zoning Ordinance.

*For those applications not required to submit a site plan, a copy of the deed, plat of the property or other legal description of the land and buildings (ie. lease agreements) will be accepted. However, further details may be required, on a case by case basis.
** For home employment uses, the umber of required and provided parking spaces can be shown by hand drawing on the copy of the record plat.

Figure 2.2   *(continued from previous page)* Sample provisional use application package

PROVISIONAL USE PERMIT FEE SCHEDULE
(As of July 1998)

Agriculture/Residential - $100.00

Home Employment Provisional Uses --
    Administrative offices of business and/or trade
    Arts and crafts activities
    Baking/Catering (off premise service)
    Beauty salon (no tanning or toning equipment)
    Clerical/secretarial activities
    Day-time adult care (no more than five adults not residing in the home)
    Diaper/laundry service
    Floral design
    Interior design/decorating
    Jewelry, watch, clock repair; engraving; locksmith; eyeglass; framing; dentures
    Maid service (off premise)
    Mail order
    Nail sculpture, manicurist
    Office of a physician, therapist (including psychological, physical, and/or massage), dentist, lawyer, accountant, engineer, architect, desktop publishing, or similar professional
    Pet grooming
    Photography
    Picture framing
    Scissor, saw, blade sharpening
    Seamstress, tailoring, upholstery activities
    Small electronics repair
    Tutoring, education or training (no more than five children or two adults at any one time)

COMMUNITY/COMMERCIAL -- $500.00

    Commercial recreation facility - indoor
    Commercial recreation facility - outdoor
    Ground level helistop
    Private recreation facility
    Quick service food store
    Restaurant drive-in
    Restaurant limited service
    Taxi and limousine dispatching

INDUSTRIAL/MISCELLANEOUS -- $1,000.00

Figure 2.2 *(continued from previous page)* Sample provisional use application package

Ambulance service facility
Company vehicle facility
Contract vehicle sales
Equipment storage
Motor vehicle parts with service-limited
Radio, TV, microwave tower
Recycling collection point
Taxi/limo operations and service facility
Watchman's dwelling

NOTE: Option upon denial of provisional use application --
              Fee for equivalent SUP minus PUP fee previously paid.

Figure 2.2 *(continued from previous page)* Sample provisional use application package

SPECIAL POWER OF ATTORNEY AFFIDAVIT

STATE OF VIRGINIA
COUNTY OF PRINCE WILLIAM

This _____ day of _____, _____,
        (day)   (month)   (year)

I, _____,
                    (owner/contract purchaser)

of _____ make, constitute, and appoint
            (describe land by tax map number)

_____, my true and lawful attorney-in-fact,
and in my name, place and stead giving unto said _____
full power and authority to do and perform all acts and make all representation
necessary, without any limitation whatsoever, to make application for said
provisional use permit.

The right, powers, and authority of said attorney-in-fact herein granted shall
commence and be in full force and effect on _____, 19_____,
and shall remain in full force and effect thereafter until actual notice, by certified
mail, return receipt requested is received by the Office of Planning of Prince
William County stating that the terms of this power have been revoked or modified.

_____
Owner/Contract Purchaser/Authorized Agent
(circle one)

COMMONWEALTH OF VIRGINIA:
County of_____
Subscribed and sworn to before me this _____ day of _____ 19_____
in my County and State aforesaid, by the aforenamed Principal.

_____
        NOTARY PUBLIC
My commission expires:_____

OFFICE USE ONLY	
File/Case number_____	Date accepted_____,19___

Figure 2.2 *(continued from previous page)* Sample provisional use application package

Prince William County, Virginia
Zoning Department

**Notification of Concurrent Processing of a provisional use permit application (PUP)
with a site/subdivision plan**

I hereby notify Prince William County that my application for a provisional use permit
requesting_____
will be processed concurrently with the site/subdivision plan. I understand that the
site/subdivision plan can not be approved or released until and unless the PUP application
has been granted approval by the Zoning Administrator. Furthermore, I understand that
the review of the site/subdivision plan will in no way prejudice the review or approval of
the PUP application, and the site/subdivision plan may need to be revised to meet
conditions associated with the PUP application. I hereby knowingly waive any claim that
the expenditure of funds used in preparation of the site/subdivision plan will provide me
and my successors or assigns any rights to the approval of said PUP application. If the
PUP application is denied by the Zoning Administrator, I understand that the
site/subdivision plan will become null and void, the plan file will be closed and no review
fees refunded.

_____   _____
Owner   Date

_____
Address

Office Use Only

PUP file #_____

Site/Subdivision #_____

Figure 2.2   *(continued from previous page)* Sample provisional use application package

TELEPHONE CONTACT LIST

Here is a list of names, telephone numbers and addresses of people you might need to contact for the Provisional Use Permit process.

For inquiry, submission and meeting
Kay Ansari – Planning Office
1 County Complex Ct.
Prince William, Va. 22192
(703) 792-6830

For Occupancy and Inspections
Building Permits/Inspections
1 County Complex Ct.
Prince William, Va. 22192
(703) 792-6924/6970

Fire Marshall Inspections
Battalion Chief Ray Scott – Fire Marshall's Office
9250 Lee Ave.
Manassas, Va. 22110
(703) 792-6360

Security Inspections
Crime Prevention Unit
Officer Dawn Harmon
15960 Cardinal Drive
Woodbridge, Va. 22191
(703) 792-7266

Deeds and Plats
Land Records @ County Courthouse
9311 Lee Ave.
Manassas, Va. 22110
(703) 792-6035

Zoning Administrator
Sherman Patrick – Planning Office
1 County Complex Ct.
Prince William, VA. 22192
(703) 792-6830

Business License
Business & Taxation Office
1 County Complex Ct.
Prince William, VA. 22192
(703) 792-6710

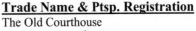

Trade Name & Ptsp. Registration
The Old Courthouse
9248 Lee Ave 1st floor
Manassas, Va. 20110
(703) 792-6045

Figure 2.2 *(continued from previous page)* Sample provisional use application package

APPLICATION FOR A PROVISIONAL USE PERMIT

Plan name:_____ PUP#:_____

Request Use:_____

TO THE ZONING ADMINISTRATOR OF PRINCE WILLIAM COUNTY, VA.

The undersigned, being all of the owner(s), contract purchasers or the respective duly authorized agents thereof, do hereby petition a provisional use permit for the property described below and shown on the accompanying plans, which are made part of this application, as follows: (Describe the proposed use and attach a copy of the conditions outlined in Section 32-230.00 of the Zoning Ordinance with your analysis of each condition.)

G.P.I.N. #	TAX MAP #	CURRENT ZONING	ACRES
_____	_____	_____	_____

Gross Floor Area:_____ Total Acres:_____

Property location (describe the location of the property by distance, in feet or portion of a mile, and direction from an intersection of two (2) public roads or streets):_____

_____

The name(s), mailing address(es), and telephone number(s) of owner(s) and contract purchaser, lessee, and/or authorized agent(s), as applicable are: (attach pages if necessary)

Owner of Property:
Name:_____
Address:_____ Phone:_____

Address of property:_____

Contract of Purchaser/Lessee:	**Authorized Agent(s):**
Name:_____	Name:_____
Address:_____	Address:_____
_____	_____
Phone:_____	Phone:_____

Signed this _____ day of _____, 19_____.

_____

Signature of Contract Purchaser/Lessee/Owner   Signature of Authorized Agent

OFFICE USE ONLY	
Magisterial District:_____	Staff Person:_____
File/Case#_____	Date accepted:_____

Figure 2.2 *(continued from previous page)* Sample provisional use application package

COUNTY OF PRINCE WILLIAM
1 County Complex Court, Prince William, Virginia 22192-9201
(703) 792-6830 Metro 631-1703, Ext. 6830 FAX (703) 792-4758
Internet www.pwcgov.org

PLANNING
OFFICE

Pre-Submission Package
for
Rezoning, Special Use Permit, and
Proffer Amendment Applications

Contents

Figure 2.3 Sample of pre-submission package *(continued on next page)*

INTRODUCTION

The items contained in this pre-submission package require completion prior to submission of a rezoning, special use permit, or proffer amendment application.

Page 3 – Request for Project Name/Number and Adjacent Property Owners List:

This form is filled out by applicants. Submit this form to the Planning Office to:

✓   Request a new or existing project name and number;

✓   Request a list of adjacent property owners. The Planning Office provides this service for a $20 fee; however, applicants have the option to generate their own list of adjacent property owners, pursuant to the requirements of Section 32-700.20(5) of the Zoning Ordinance. Should applicants choose to generate their own list, it will be necessary to include two sets of mailing labels, with the addresses on them. Regardless of how the list is generated, the applicant will be required to certify its accuracy with an affidavit submitted with the application.

Page 4 – Application for Deferral of Traffic Impact Analysis (TIA)

Complete form with assistance from the Transportation Planning Branch of the Department of Public Works (located at 4379 Ridgewood Drive; 703-792-7441) to:

✓   Assess whether or not a TIA will be required to be submitted with the application.

Staff from Transportation Planning will be present at pre-application meetings to help determine if a TIA will be necessary at the time of submittal of an application. While a TIA may not be necessary with an application, further analysis of the proposal may necessitate submittal of a TIA later in the rezoning, special use permit, or proffer amendment application process, or during the site plan review process. Either the deferral form or a TIA is required with the submission of an application.

Page 5 – Cultural Resource and Assessment Check

Complete form with assistance from the Cultural Resources Coordinator, in the Planning Office (703-792-6830) to:

✓   Assess whether or not a Phase I Archaeological Survey will be required to be submitted with the application.

✓   While not required to be submitted with a rezoning, special use permit, or proffer amendment application, the Cultural Resources Coordinator may recommend that a Phase I Archaeological Survey be submitted prior to scheduling any public hearings.

Either the form or a Phase I Survey is required with the submission of an application.

Figure 2.3 *(continued from previous page)* Sample of pre-submission package

**REQUEST FOR PROJECT NAME AND NUMBER /
ADJACENT PROPERTY OWNERS LIST**
(to be filled out by applicant)

REQUEST FOR:

o   **PROJECT NAME AND NUMBER – Required for rezoning applications.**
        Please use project name on the application.

Project Name Requested: _____

REQUEST FOR:

o   **ADJACENT PROPERTY OWNERS LIST – Optional**
        The Planning Office provides a service where an applicant may request that the Planning
        Office generate a list of adjacent property owners. There is a **$20.00 fee** for this service.
        Checks should be made payable to Prince William County.

        The applicant should review this list to ensure that it includes property owners within 200
        feet of the property, including subject property and all property immediately across the
        street or road from the subject property; and nearby homeowners and/or civic
        associations within 2,000 feet of the property, as well as jurisdictions within ½ mile of
        the subject property. Adjacent property owners lists can be e-mailed to the applicant for
        proofing and editing. *The list and the adjacent property owners affidavit must be
        returned with the completed application package.*

For the property described below (proposals for multiple parcels should also include a copy of
the plat):

G.P.I.N. #		Acres:

Please indicate to whom response should be sent:

name:_____   e-mail: _____

address: _____   phone: _____

Figure 2.3 *(continued from previous page)* Sample of pre-submission package

APPLICATION FOR DEFERRAL OF TRAFFIC IMPACT ANALYSIS (TIA)
(to be completed with assistance from Transportation Planning; see Page 2)

To be completed by applicant:

Applicant Name: _____ Phone: _____

Proposed Use: _____

Location: _____ Lot Size: _____

Check one:

❏   Rezoning   ❏   Special Use Permit   ❏   Other _____

Proposed Land Use/Trip Generation:

To be completed by applicant:				To be completed by Transportation Planning:				
Tract/Use	Area	Zoning	Land Use	ITE Code	(ITE Latest Edition Trip Rate)	Trips/24 Hours	Trips/AM Peak	Trips/PM Peak
			Total					
		100 Directional Trips			Yes			
					No			

FOR OFFICE USE ONLY

☐   A TIA is required to be submitted with the application. The consultant preparing the analysis must meet with the Public Works Transportation Planning Section to discuss the scope and requirements of the analysis before beginning the analysis.

☐   A TIA is not required to be submitted with the application. The traffic generated by the proposal does not appear to exceed the thresholds established in §602.01 of the Design and Construction Standards Manual. However, **a TIA may be required later in the rezoning/special use permit process or during the site plan review process if subsequent details warrant a TIA.**

☐   A TIA has been waived by the Director for the following reasons:

_____

_____

Signature of Public Works Transportation Reviewer: _____

Reviewed by: _____ Date: _____

Figure 2.3 *(continued from previous page)* Sample of pre-submission package

CULTURAL RESOURCE ASSESSMENT AND RECORD CHECK FOR PENDING DEVELOPMENT APPLICATIONS
(to be completed with assistance from Planning Office staff; see Page 2)

Project Name: _____

1. Visual Inspection Findings: (*Describe what is on the property now, the date the inspection was performed, and the method used*): _____

_____

_____

2. County Records Check: (*Verify whether any reference is contained on this site on the following sources*):

Prince William County Cultural Resources Map (GIS)	Yes_____	No_____
1820 Prince William County Map (Wood)	Yes_____	No_____
1901 Prince William County Map (Brown)	Yes_____	No_____
1904 Army Maneuvers Map	Yes_____	No_____
1933 Virginia Highway Map	Yes_____	No_____
Eugene Scheel's Historic Prince William Map	Yes_____	No_____
Eugene Scheel's African American Heritage Map	Yes_____	No_____
*Designated Cultural Resource	Yes_____	No_____
*High Sensitivity Areas – Historic Sites Map	Yes_____	No_____
*High Sensitivity Areas – Prehistoric Sites Map	Yes_____	No_____
The Official Military Atlas of the Civil War	Yes_____	No_____
Civil War Map from the Library of Congress	Yes_____	No_____

*If "Yes", a Phase I Archeology Survey must be submitted with Rezoning and Special Use Permit applications, per Sections 32-700.20(9) and 32-700.50(3)(a) of the Zoning Ordinance.

3. Discussion:
   (*Discuss specifics whenever a "yes" box has been checked*)

_____

_____

_____

4. Conclusion: (Explain as necessary on separate sheet)

_____ No known historical sites or gravesites were found on site or would be suspected by a reasonable person to be found on site.

_____ Although historical sites or gravesites were found on or near site, development will not impact.

_____ Historical sites and/or gravesites are located on or adjacent to the site, and will be protected.

Applicant's Signature and Title: _____   Date: _____

Cultural Resources Coordinator Signature: _____   Date: _____

Figure 2.3 *(continued from previous page)* Sample of pre-submission package

COUNTY OF PRINCE WILLIAM
1 County Complex Court, Prince William, Virginia 22192-9201
(703) 792-6830 Metro 631-1703, Ext. 6830 FAX (703) 792-4758
Internet www.pwcgov.org

PLANNING
OFFICE

Application Package
for
Rezonings and Proffer Amendments

Contents

Figure 2.4 Application package for rezoning and proffer amendments *(continued on next page)*

INSTRUCTIONS

All items contained in this application package must be completed and submitted with the supplemental items identified in the reference manual. Additional information may be requested during the pre-application conference. **Please attach additional pages where necessary to identify all requested information clearly.**

Page 2 – Application for a Rezoning / Proffer Amendment (required)

✓ Fill in the project name and number (pre-submission requirement).
✓ Identify the rezoning or proffer amendment request.
✓ Describe the property location.
✓ Give names of the owner of the property, authorized agent(s), contract purchaser/lessee, and engineer. Please check the box next to the contact person to whom correspondence on the application should be sent.
✓ Sign application. If the owner(s) of the property does not sign the application, a power of attorney must be submitted indicating; see page 6.

Page 3 – Fee Calculation Worksheet (required)

✓ Complete form based on the attached fee schedule.

Page 4 – Request for Modification or Waiver of Standards

✓ Complete form if a modification or waiver of standards is proposed as part of the rezoning or proffer amendment request. Only those provisions of the Zoning Ordinance that may be waived by the Board of County Supervisors may be listed on this form.

Page 5 – Interest Disclosure Affidavit (required)

✓ This form is required to disclose whether or not any member of the Planning Commission or Board of County Supervisors has greater than ten percent interest in the company, or relating to the proposal. Must be signed by the property owner(s).

Page 6 – Special Power of Attorney Affidavit

✓ This form is required if someone other than the property owner(s) is signing the application and other documents requiring the property owner(s) signature.

Page 7 – Adjacent Property Owners Affidavit (required)

✓ The adjacent property owners list (which may be requested with the pre-submission package) must be certified by the property owner(s) as being accurate and fulfilling the requirements of Section 32-700.20(5) of the Zoning Ordinance.

Page 8 – Fee Schedule

Figure 2.4 *(continued from previous page)* Application package for rezoning and proffer amendments

APPLICATION FOR A REZONING / PROFFER AMENDMENT (circle one)

TO THE BOARD OF COUNTY SUPERVISORS OF PRINCE WILLIAM COUNTY, VIRGINIA

Project Name _____ **Project Number** _____

The undersigned, being all of the owner(s), contract purchasers, or the respective duly authorized agents thereof, do hereby petition to change the zoning of the property described below and shown on the accompanying plans, which are made part of this application, as follows:

G.P.I.N. #   **From:**   **To:**   **Acres:**   (Total) _____

_____   _____   _____   _____

_____   _____   _____   _____

- OR -

The undersigned propose(s) to amend the proffered conditions of
Rezoning # _____

Property Location (Describe the location of the property by distance, in feet or portion of a mile, and direction from an intersection of two (2) public roads or streets.

_____

_____

The name(s), mailing address(es), and telephone number(s) of owner(s), authorized agent(s), contract purchaser/lessee, and engineer(s) as applicable are:

❑ **Owner of Property**   ❑ **Authorized Agent(s)**

name:_____   name:_____
mailing _____   mailing: _____
address: _____   address: _____
phone: _____   phone: _____

❑ **Contract Purchaser/Lessee**   ❑ **Engineer**

name:_____   name:_____
mailing _____   mailing _____
address: _____   address: _____
phone: _____   phone: _____

Please check the box next to the contact to which correspondence should be sent.

I have read this application, understand its intent, and freely consent to its filing. Furthermore, I have the power to authorize and hereby grant permission to Prince William County officials and other authorized government agents on official business to enter the property as necessary to process this application.

Signed this _____ day of _____, _____.

_____
Signature of Owner
(If anyone other than owner is signing, power of attorney must be attached.)

Figure 2.4 *(continued from previous page)* Application package for rezoning and proffer amendments

FEE CALCULATION WORKSHEET:

Base Rate: =$_____
(if proposing multiple zoning
categories, enter highest rate)

Per/Acre Rate: $_____ X _____   =$_____
                                                                              (# acres)

Additional Per/Acre Rate: $_____ X _____   =$_____
(if proposing multiple zoning   (# acres)
categories)

Additional Per/Acre Rate: $_____ X _____   =$_____
(if proposing multiple zoning   (# acres)
categories)

Additional Per/Acre Rate: $_____ X _____   =$_____
(if proposing multiple zoning   (# acres)
categories)

Additional Per/Acre Rate: _____ X $_____   =$_____
(if proposing multiple zoning   (# acres)
categories)

Service Authority Review Fee   =$
(if located within service area):

                                                                    Total =$ [_____]

Figure 2.4 *(continued from previous page)* Application package for rezoning and proffer amendments

REQUEST FOR MODIFICATION OR WAIVER OF STANDARDS

Whenever any standard imposed by any provision of the Zoning Ordinance or other County ordinance may be waived or modified by proffer approved by the Board of County Supervisors, this form must accompany an application for rezoning for such waiver or modification, and may constitute the whole of or a part of such application.

Applicant:_____

Case Name:_____

Please indicate the requested modification(s) or waiver(s) below. Attach a written statement describing the requested modification or waiver, referencing the citation, and providing justification for the request.

❑ Waiver of specific requirements of the Subdivision Ordinance, Zoning Ordinance, or DCSM as it relates to Planned Districts. See Section 32-280.07 of the Zoning Ordinance.

❑ Waiver of specific requirements of the Subdivision Ordinance, Zoning Ordinance, or DCSM as it relates to an RPC. See Section 32-305.02 of the Zoning Ordinance.

Modification of development standards:

❑ Building Height
❑ Floor Area Ratio (FAR)
❑ Signs

See Sections 32-300.05, 32-400.03, 32-400.04 or 32-250.24 of the Zoning Ordinance

Modification of development standards in B-3 zoning district:

❑ Reduction in minimum lot size
❑ Reduction in minimum district size

See Section 32-401.36 of the Zoning Ordinance

Figure 2.4 *(continued from previous page)* Application package for rezoning and proffer amendments

INTEREST DISCLOSURE AFFIDAVIT

STATE OF VIRGINIA
COUNTY OF PRINCE WILLIAM

This _____ day of _____, _____,
       (Day)   (Month)   (Year)

I, _____(Owner)

hereby make oath that no member of the Board of County Supervisors of the County of Prince William, Virginia, nor the Planning Commission of the County of Prince William, Virginia, has interest in such property, either individually, by ownership of stock in a corporation owning such land, or partnership, or as holder of ten (10) percent or more of the outstanding shares of stock in or as a director or officer of any corporation owning such land, directly or indirectly, by such member or members of his immediate household, except as follows:

_____

_____

_____

_____

_____
                                   Owner

COMMONWEALTH OF VIRGINIA:

County of _____

Subscribed and sworn to before me this _____ day of _____, _____ in my county and state aforesaid, by the aforenamed principal.

_____
                       NOTARY PUBLIC

My Commission Expires: _____

Figure 2.4 *(continued from previous page)* Application package for rezoning and proffer amendments

SPECIAL POWER OF ATTORNEY AFFIDAVIT

STATE OF VIRGINIA
COUNTY OF PRINCE WILLIAM

This _____ day of _____, _____,
          (Day)   (Month)   (Year)

I, _____, the owner of

_____ (describe land by parcel identification number

[PIN]) make, constitute, and appoint _____,

my true and lawful attorney-in-fact, and in my name, place and stead giving unto said

_____ full power and authority to do and perform

all acts and make all representation necessary, without any limitation whatsoever, to make

application for said rezoning.

The right, powers, and authority of said attorney-in-fact herein granted shall commence and be in

full force and effect on _____, _____, and shall remain in full force

and effect thereafter until actual notice, by certified mail, return receipt requested is received by

the Office of Planning of Prince William County stating that the terms of this power have been

revoked or modified.

_____
                               Owner

COMMONWEALTH OF VIRGINIA:

County of _____

Subscribed and sworn to before me this _____ day of _____, _____ in my county
and state aforesaid, by the aforenamed principal.

_____
                         NOTARY PUBLIC

My Commission Expires: _____

Figure 2.4 *(continued from previous page)* Application package for rezoning and proffer amendments

ADJACENT PROPERTY OWNERS AFFIDAVIT

STATE OF VIRGINIA
COUNTY OF PRINCE WILLIAM

This _____ day of _____, _____,
       (Day)   (Month)   (Year)

I, _____
          (Owner/Contract Purchaser/Authorized Agent)
hereby make oath that the list of landowners within 200 feet of all portions of the subject property, including the subject property, all property immediately across the street or road from the subject property, those parcels which lie in other localities of the Commonwealth, any homeowners and/or civic associations having jurisdiction over the property or within 2,000 feet of all portions of the subject property, jurisdictions located within one-half mile of all portions of the subject property, and the appropriate state or federal agency if a state or federally owned facility is within one-half mile of all portions of the subject property, is a true and accurate list as submitted with my application.

                                           _____
                                         Owner/Contract Purchaser/Authorized Agent
                                         (circle one)

COMMONWEALTH OF VIRGINIA:

County of _____

Subscribed and sworn to before me this _____ day of _____, _____ in my county and state aforesaid, by the aforenamed principal.

                                         _____
                                           NOTARY PUBLIC

My Commission Expires: _____

Figure 2.4 *(continued from previous page)* Application package for rezoning and proffer amendments

REZONING / PROFFER AMENDMENT FEE SCHEDULE
Effective July 1, 2003

	Zoning District	Base Rate	Plus/Acre
A-1	Agricultural	$1,962.00	
RR-7.5	Rural Residential	$1,962.00	$50.00
RR- 5	Rural Residential	$1,962.00	$70.00
SRR-3	Semi-rural Residential	$1,962.00	$85.00
SRR-1	Semi-rural Residential	$1,962.00	$95.00
R-20	Suburban Residential	$1,962.00	$100.00
R-10	Suburban Residential	$1,962.00	$105.00
RD-	Residential Duplex	$3,270.00	$110.00
SR-6	Suburban Residential	$3,270.00	$125.00
RMH	Residential Mobile Home	$3,270.00	$100.00
RM-1	Urban Residential	$3,270.00	$140.00
RM-2	Urban Residential	$3,270.00	$140.00
RE	Residential Elderly	$3,270.00	$140.00
PMR	Planned Mixed Residential	$4,900.00	$140.00
PMR	Addition	$4,900.00	$140.00
PMR	Amendment	$3,270.00	$140.00
RPC	Residential Planned Community	$4,900.00	$140.00
RPC	Addition	$4,900.00	$140.00
RPC	Amendment	$3,270.00	$140.00
B-1	General Business	$3,270.00	$120.00
B-2	Neighborhood Business	$3,270.00	$100.00
B-3	Convenience Retail	$3,270.00	$100.00
B-R	Regional Business	$4,900.00	$140.00
O(L)	Office – Low-rise	$3,270.00	$100.00
O(M)	Office – Mid-rise	$3,270.00	$135.00
O(H)	Office – High-rise	$3,270.00	$175.00
O(F)	Office – Flex	$3,270.00	$135.00
M-1	Heavy Industrial	$3,270.00	$155.00
M-2	Light Industrial	$3,270.00	$130.00
M-T	Industrial/Transportation	$3,270.00	$175.00
PBD	Planned Business District	$6,540.00	$195.00
PBD	Addition	$6,540.00	$195.00
PBD	Amendment	$3,270.00	$195.00

Figure 2.4 *(continued from previous page)* Application package for rezoning and proffer amendments

PMD	Planned Mixed Use District	$6,540.00	$200.00 for first 500 acres; $100.00 for 501-1,000 acres (in addition to fee for first 500 acres) $50.00 for 1,001 – 1,500 acres(in addition to fees for first 1,000 acres) $25.00 for 1,501 acres and above(in addition to fees for first 1,500 acres)
PMD	Addition	$6,540.00	$205.00
PMD	Amendment	$3,270.00	$205.00

	Other Fees	
	Service Authority Review – Required for most rezoning applications	$40.00
	Rezoning of less than 40,000 sq. ft. in land area to a residential use (does not create new lots)	$1,962.00
	Corrective rezoning of less than 40,000 sq. ft. in land area	$1,962.00
	Proffer Amendment – not involving significant modifications to the basic submission or general development plan. Substantive changes to proffered conditions require a new zoning application	$1,962.00

Refunds:

A refund of 25% of the application fee shall be returned to the applicant if the rezoning application is withdrawn prior to the submission of a newspaper advertisement announcing the Planning Commission public hearing. Cases withdrawn after the advertisement will not have any funds reimbursed.

Figure 2.4 *(continued from previous page)* Application package for rezoning and proffer amendments

Effective: August 8, 1994

PRINCE WILLIAM COUNTY OFFICE OF PLANNING

PLAN NAME: _____

<u>CO - SIGNATURE SUBMISSION CHECKLIST</u>

CODE	ADMINISTRATIVE ITEMS	Number Of Copies	YES	NO	N/A
C 01	Number of plans				
C 02	Are plans legible?				
C 03	Number of separate plats- mylar, mylar sepia original and blackline/blueline copies				
C 04	Plats legible (signature/seals)?				
C 05	Notary complete to include county and state				
C 06	Title of person signing plat legible?				
C 07	Appropriate maintenance notes for all easements on the plats				
C 08	If signature submission is a revision to an approved plan, plans must be circled in red				
C 09	Site Development Permit Calculation Sheet				
C 10	Signed Unit Price List for bonds and escrows				
C 11	Storm Water Management Fact Sheet (required if pond is part of plan)				
C 12	Response letter from submitting engineer addressing all outstanding agency comments, and the Plan Analysis comments identified in the Summary Letter				
C 13	Copies of Summary Letter and Agency Comments				
C 14	One copy of plan circled in green addressing all outstanding agency comments				
C 15	Proffer Analysis/Special Use Permit Analysis is included in the plan/booklet				
C 16	Submission of appropriate number copies of computations if required and not included as part of the plan sheets (Floodplain, SWM/BMP)				
C 17	Executed, original deeds with deed checklist must be submitted with each plan/plat signature submission. For each plat, a deed will be required to be included in the signature submission unless plat is a sanitary sewer plat <u>only</u>. Deeds for these types of easements are not required to be submitted to the Office of Planning, but to the Service Authority, Dale Service Corporation or the Virginia American Water Company, whichever are applicable. Deds are also not required for resubdivisions or 466K subdivisions if no rights-of-way or easements are being conveyed to the Board of County Supervisors.				

I HEREBY CERTIFY THAT THE STATED INFORMATION IS INCLUDED IN THE ATTACHED PLAN AND/OR DOCUMENTS.

DATE:_____   _____

                                       Engineer/Surveyor Signature

Signature Submission Checklist

Checklist 2.9   Co-signature submission checklist

PRINCE WILLIAM COUNTY OFFICE OF PLANNING

PLAN NAME: _____

PRESUBMISSION/SKETCH PLAN
MINIMUM SUBMISSION REQUIREMENTS CHECKLIST

CEM CODE	ADMINISTRATIVE ITEMS	Admin. Procedures Section	YES	NO	N/A
E01	Fees in accordance with the Fee Schedule. A certified Prince William County (PWC) Review Fee Calculation Sheet.	4.05.1(A)			
E02	Standard Prince William County Development Control Form with all required information. (If not signed by the owner, a Power of Attorney must accompany this form.)	4.05.2(A1)			
	PLAN DETAILS				
E03	Sheet size not to exceed 36" x 48" (900 millimeters x 1,219 millimeters). More than two sheets indexed with match lines following lot lines for lots of five acres (2.02 hectares) or less in size.	4.05.2(B1)			
E04	A scale of no less than 1" = 200' (metric ratio 1:2,000).	4.05.2(B2)			
E05	Contour interval no greater than 5' (1.52 meters) referenced USGS Datum.	4.05.2(B3)			
E06	Date of plan, north arrow match lines, and sheet numbers.	4.05.2(B4)			
E07	Vicinity map, preferably at 1" = 2000' (metric ratio (1:25,000), but not smaller than 1" = 3000' (metric ratio 1:50,000).	4.05.2(B5)			
E08	Present zoning of the project parcel(s) and all adjacent parcels, along with their present use. Provide the project name and plan number of adjacent development as assigned by PWC, if applicable.	4.05.2(B6)			
E09	The project parcel(s) GPIN and all adjacent parcels' GPINs or GSINs.	4.05.2(B7)			
E10	Total project site acreage (hectares).	4.05.2(B8)			
E11	The generalized proposed pattern of lots and/or buildings (including number and size, street layout, off-street parking, recreation areas, open space, improvements to existing streets and rights-of-ways, buffers, vehicles per day, and storm water management facilities.	4.05.2(B9)			
E12	Existing easements, covenants and any other restriction shown.	4.05.1(B10)			
E13	Existing drainage facilities, including major culverts, ponds and streams.	4.05.2(B11)			
E14	Location of all existing situations and buildings on-site.	4.05.2(B12)			
E15	Note on plan stating the following: "This plan has not been reviewed for conformance with rezoning proffers and/or special use permit conditions, if applicable. These will be reviewed with the final plan submission."	4.05.2(B13)			

I HEREBY CERTIFY THAT THE STATED INFORMATION IS INCLUDED IN THE ATTACHED PLAN.

DATE:_____   _____
                                        Engineer/Surveyor Signature

ce:land:chklist2

Checklist 2.10   Checklist for pre-submission sketch plans

CITY OF CLEARWATER
PLANNING & DEVELOPMENT SERVICES
100 S. Myrtle Avenue, Clearwater, FL 33756
Phone (727) 562-4567   Fax (727) 562-4576

LANDSCAPE PLAN REQUIREMENTS

ADDRESS _____

Except in the Tourist and Downtown Districts, landscaping shall be required in accordance with the provisions of Article 3 Division 12 for the following development:

1. All development and the redevelopment or reconfiguration of an surface off-street parking facility.
2. All development within designated scenic corridors.
3. The expansion of the floor area of an existing nonresidential or multifamily structure.

Your plans will not be processed if any of the items listed below are incomplete or missing. An application for any proposed work becomes void if a permit is not issued within six (6) months of the date submitted. A plans review fee is due upon submittal.

Three (3) copies of the landscape plan must be submitted showing the following information:

___   1. All proposed structure and improvements, including but not limited to walls, fences, walks, pools, patios, dumpster pads, pad mounted transformers, fire hydrants, overhead obstructions, easements, sign locations, treatment of all ground surfaces, and any other features that may influence the proposed landscape;

___   2. Name of abutting street rights-of-way;

___   3. Drainage and retention areas, including swales, side slopes and bottom elevations, and drainage structures and other drainage improvements;

___   4. Delineation and dimensions of all required perimeter landscape buffers including sight triangles, if any;

___   5. Delineation of parking areas and other vehicular use areas, including parking spaces, circulation aisles, interior landscape islands and curbing;

___   6. Proposed and required parking spaces;

___   7. Existing trees on site and immediately adjacent to the site, by species, size and location, including dripline;

___   8. Location, size, description, specification and quantities of all existing and proposed landscape materials, including botanical and common names;

___   9. Typical planting details for trees, palms, shrubs, and ground cover plants, including planting instructions, soil mixes, backfilling, mulching, staking and protective measures;

___ 10. Interior landscape areas hatched and/or shaded and labeled and interior landscape coverage, expressed both in square feet , exclusive of perimeter landscape strips, and as a percentage of the paved area coverage of the parking lot and vehicular use areas;

___ 11. An irrigation plan for all development requiring Level Two and Three approval;

___ 12. Any conditions of development approval;

___ 13. Any other information that may be needed to show compliance with the provisions of Article 3 Division 12.

Figure 2.5   Landscape plan requirements *(continued on next page)*

For Sites one acre or greater in size or sites having 150' or more of street frontage, the following information is required:

__ 1. A scaled drawing showing the finished elevation of all landscape material proposed to be planted with perimeter landscape buffers adjacent to street rights-of-way. The drawing shall be an artistic rendering of the proposed landscape material as it will appear at the time of installation and will provide a "snapshot" of the overall appearance of the landscape material. The drawing shall include a rendering of all trees, shrubs and groundcovers and should include structures such as walls, fences, signage, benches, utility poles or other structures with the required buffers;

__ 2. Dimensional measurements showing the height from finished grade of all landscape materials utilized in the landscape buffers.

Please return check list for review and verification.

Date: _____   _____
                                                          (signature of applicant)

Figure 2.5 *(continued from previous page)* Landscape plan requirements

COUNTY OF PRINCE WILLIAM
1 County Complex Court, Prince William, Virginia 22192-9201
(703) 792-6830   Metro 631-1703   Fax: (703) 792-4758

PLANNING
OFFICE

Stephen K. Griffin,
AICP
Director of Planning

COMPREHENSIVE PLAN AMENDMENTS

November 13, 2003

Dear Applicant:

Each year, the Prince William Board of County Supervisors reviews requests for amendments to the Comprehensive Plan and initiates those proposed amendments that they feel merit consideration.

Applications for Comprehensive Plan amendment consideration in 2004 must be received in the Planning Office no later than close of business on Friday, January 2, 2004. A copy of the application form is attached. Please read the entire application, including the Attachment, and respond in full to those questions that pertain to the particular map or text amendment you are requesting. Incomplete applications shall not be considered. CPA applications will not be accepted after this date.

If you have any questions, please contact Ray Utz of the Planning Office at (703) 792-6830.

Figure 2.6   Sample request form for plans amendment *(continued on next page)*

2003 COMPREHENSIVE PLAN AMENDMENT
INITIATION REQUEST FORM
(Please type all information. The application will not be deemed complete unless all items listed below have been submitted.)

A.   Owner or Authorized Agent information:

    1.   Name: _____

    2.   Project Name: _____

    3.   Mailing Address: _____

                         _____

    4.   Telephone Number: _____

B.   Legal interest in the property affected or reason for the request:

    _____

C.   Proposed Comprehensive Plan amendment – please provide the following information.

1.   For a map amendment:

    a.   GPIN(s): _____

    b.   Parcel size (approximate acres):_____

    c.   Plat of area proposed for CPA amendment, including metes and bounds description. The plat should be prepared pursuant to Section 32-700.20 of the Zoning Ordinance.

    d.   Existing Comprehensive Plan land use classification(s):_____

        _____

    e.   Proposed Comprehensive Plan land use classification(s):_____

        _____

    f.   Existing zoning and land use of the subject parcel:_____

Figure 2.6 *(continued from previous page)* Sample request form for plans amendment

g. What use/zoning will be requested if amendment is approved?

_____

_____

h. Describe (using text, photos, and maps as necessary) the existing zoning, Comprehensive Plan designations, and/or approved uses and densities along with other characteristics of area within:

- 1/4 mile from the parcel(s) perimeter if the parcel is less than 20 acres in size;

- 1/2 mile if 21-100 acres in size; or

- 1 mile if more than 100 acres in size.

i. The name, mailing address, and parcel number of all property owners within 200 ft. of the subject parcel(s) (with Adjacent Property Owners Affidavit [see page 7]).

j. Cultural Resource Assessment and Record Check. (See page 10.)

k. Traffic impact analysis (or deferral by Public Works, Transportation) (see page 9 of application packet); and

l. Description of Environmental Resources (ER) on the property.

2.   For a text amendment:

a. Purpose and intent of amendment

b. Cite Plan chapter, goal, policy and/or action strategy text that is proposed to be amended.

c. Proposed new or revised text.

(Note: Please attach and specify text changes with additions underlined and deletions crossed through.)

d. Demonstrate how the proposal furthers the goals, policies/objectives, and action strategies set forth in the Comprehensive Plan chapter(s) relative to the amendment request and why proposed revisions to said goals, policies, and action strategies are appropriate.

_____

e. Demonstrate how the proposal is internally consistent with other Comprehensive Plan components that are not the subject of the amendment.

Figure 2.6   *(continued from previous page)* Sample request form for plans amendment

f.   What level of service impacts, if any, are associated with the request?

_____

3.   For all amendments:

a.   Justification of proposed Comprehensive Plan amendment (provide attachments if necessary). Describe why the change to the Comprehensive Plan is being proposed.

_____

_____

b.   How would the resultant changes impact or benefit Prince William County relative to:

1.   Community Design

2.   Cultural Resources

3.   Economic Development

4.   Environment

5.   Fire and Rescue

6.   Housing

7.   Land Use

8.   Libraries

9.   Parks and Open Space

10.   Potable Water

11.   Schools

12.   Sewer

13.   Telecommunications

Figure 2.6   *(continued from previous page)* Sample request form for plans amendment

14. Transportation

15. Sector Plan (if applicable)

D. Other information as may be required by the Director of Planning, the Planning Commission, or Board of County Supervisors during the review of the initiation request. The applicant will be notified, in writing, if additional information is required.

All applications must also contain the following forms:

1. Special Power of Attorney Affidavit
2. Interest Disclosure Affidavit
3. Adjacent Owners Affidavit
4. Subject Property Owner's Affidavit

Applicants should consult the Comprehensive Plan to identify goals, policies or action strategies which are applicable to individual Comprehensive Plan amendment requests.

Attachments

August 2003

Figure 2.6 *(continued from previous page)* Sample request form for plans amendment

SPECIAL POWER OF ATTORNEY AFFIDAVIT

STATE OF VIRGINIA
COUNTY OF PRINCE WILLIAM

This _____ day of _____, _____,
           (Day)   (Month)   (Year)

I, _____, the owner of

_____ (describe land by Parcel Identification Number)

make, constitute, and appoint _____,

my true and lawful attorney-in-fact, and in my name, place and stead giving unto said

_____ full power and authority to do and perform

all acts and make all representation necessary, without any limitation whatsoever, to make

application for said rezoning.

The right, powers, and authority of said attorney-in-fact herein granted shall commence and be in

full force and effect on _____, _____, and shall remain in full force

and effect thereafter until actual notice, by certified mail, return receipt requested is received by

the Office of Planning of Prince William County stating that the terms of this power have been

revoked or modified.

_____
                                      Owner

COMMONWEALTH OF VIRGINIA:

County of _____

Subscribed and sworn to before me this _____ day of _____, _____ in my County
and State aforesaid, by the aforenamed Principal.

_____
                          NOTARY PUBLIC

My Commission expires: _____

Figure 2.6 *(continued from previous page)* Sample request form for plans amendment

INTEREST DISCLOSURE AFFIDAVIT

STATE OF VIRGINIA
COUNTY OF PRINCE WILLIAM

This _____ day of _____, _____,
      (Day)   (Month)   (Year)

I, _____(Owner)

hereby make oath that no member of the Board of County Supervisors of the County of Prince

William, Virginia, nor the Planning Commission of the County of Prince William, Virginia has

interest in such property, either individually, by ownership of stock in a corporation owning such

land, or partnership, or as holder of ten (10) percent or more of the outstanding shares of stock in

or as a director or officer of any corporation owning such land, directly or indirectly, by such

member or members of his immediate household, except as follows:

_____

_____

_____

_____

                                           _____
                                                Owner

COMMONWEALTH OF VIRGINIA:

County of _____

Subscribed and sworn to before me this _____ day of _____, _____ in my County
and State aforesaid, by the aforenamed Principal.

                                           _____
                                          NOTARY PUBLIC

My Commission expires: _____

Figure 2.6 *(continued from previous page)* Sample request form for plans amendment

ADJACENT PROPERTY OWNERS AFFIDAVIT

STATE OF VIRGINIA
COUNTY OF PRINCE WILLIAM

This _____ day of _____, _____,
        (Day)   (Month)   (Year)

I, _____
               (Owner/Contract Purchaser/Authorized Agent)

hereby make oath that the list of landowners within 200 feet of all portions of the subject property, including the subject property, all property immediately across the street or road from the subject property, those parcels which lie in other localities of the Commonwealth, any homeowner's and/or civic associations having jurisdiction over the property or within 2,000 feet of all portions of the subject property, jurisdictions located within one-half mile of all portions of the subject property, and the appropriate state or federal agency if a state or federally owned facility is within one-half mile of all portions of the subject property, is a true and accurate list as submitted with my application.

_____
Owner/Contract Purchaser/Authorized Agent
(circle one)

COMMONWEALTH OF VIRGINIA:

County of _____

Subscribed and sworn to before me this _____ day of _____, _____ in my County and State aforesaid, by the aforenamed Principal.

_____
                         NOTARY PUBLIC

My Commission expires: _____

Figure 2.6 *(continued from previous page)* Sample request form for plans amendment

SUBJECT PROPERTY OWNERS AFFIDAVIT

COMMONWEALTH OF VIRGINIA
COUNTY OF PRINCE WILLIAM

This _____ day of _____, _____,
       (Day)   (Month)   (Year)

I, _____
          (Owner/Contract Purchaser/Authorized Agent)

hereby make oath that the list of property owners of the subject site, as submitted with the

application, is a true and accurate list based on the information provided by the Prince William

County Mapping Office as taken from the current real estate assessment records.

                             _____

                             Owner/Contract Purchaser/Authorized Agent
                                     (circle one)

COMMONWEALTH OF VIRGINIA:

County of _____

Subscribed and sworn to before me this _____ day of _____, _____ in my County
and State aforesaid, by the aforenamed Principal.

                             _____

                                    NOTARY PUBLIC

My Commission expires: _____

Figure 2.6 *(continued from previous page)* Sample request form for plans amendment

APPLICATION FOR DEFERRAL OF TRAFFIC IMPACT ANALYSIS (TIA)
(to be completed with assistance from Plannin g Office staff; see Page 2)

To be completed by applicant

Applicant Name:_____ Phone:_____

Proposed Use:_____

Location:_____ Lot Size:_____

Check one:
☐ Rezoning   ☐ Special Use Permit   ☐ Other_____

EXISTING LAND USE PLAN

To be completed by applicant:				To be completed by Transportation Planning:				
Tract/Use	Area	Zoning	Land Use	ITE Code	(ITE Latest Edition Trip Rate)	Trips/24 Hours	Trips/AM Peak	Trips/PM Peak
.		N/A					N/A	N/A
						Total		

PROPOSED LAND USE PLAN

To be completed by applicant:				To be completed by Transportation Planning:				
Tract/Use	Area	Zoning	Land Use	ITE Code	(ITE Latest Edition Trip Rate)	Trips/24 Hours	Trips/AM Peak	Trips/PM Peak
		N/A					N/A	N/A
						Total		

FOR OFFICE USE ONLY

☐ A TIA is required to be submitted with the application. The consultant preparing the study must meet with the Public Works Transportation Planning Section to discuss the scope and requirements of the analysis before beginning the analysis.

☐ A TIA is not required to be submitted with the application. The traffic generated by the proposal does not appear to exceed the thresholds established in §602.01 of the Design and Construction Standards Manual. However, **a TIA may be required later in the rezoning/special use permit process or during the site plan review process if subsequent details warrant a TIA.**

☐ A TIA has been waived by the Director for the following reasons:

_____

_____

Signature of Public Works Transportation Reviewer: _____

Reviewed by: _____ Date: _____

Figure 2.6 *(continued from previous page)* Sample request form for plans amendment

CULTURAL RESOURCE ASSESSMENT AND RECORD CHECK FOR PENDING DEVELOPMENT APPLICATIONS
(to be completed with assistance from Planning Office staff; see Page 2)

Project Name: _____

1. Visual Inspection Findings: (*Describe what is on the property now, the date the inspection was performed, and the method used*): _____

_____

_____

2. County Records Check: (*Verify whether any reference is contained on this site on the following sources*):

Prince William County Cultural Resources Map (GIS)	Yes_____	No_____
1820 Prince William County Map (Wood)	Yes_____	No_____
1901 Prince William County Map (Brown)	Yes_____	No_____
1904 Army Maneuvers Map	Yes_____	No_____
1933 Virginia Highway Map	Yes_____	No_____
Eugene Scheel's Historic Prince William Map	Yes_____	No_____
Eugene Scheel's African American Heritage Map	Yes_____	No_____
*Designated Cultural Resource	Yes_____	No_____
*High Sensitivity Areas – Historic Sites Map	Yes_____	No_____
*High Sensitivity Areas – Prehistoric Sites Map	Yes_____	No_____
The Official Military Atlas of the Civil War	Yes_____	No_____
Civil War Map from the Library of Congress	Yes_____	No_____

*If "Yes", a Phase I Archeology Survey must be submitted with Rezoning and Special Use Permit applications, per Sections 32-700.20(9) and 32-700.50(3)(a) of the Zoning Ordinance.

3. Discussion:
(*Discuss specifics whenever a "yes" box has been checked*)

_____

_____

_____

4. Conclusion: (Explain as necessary on separate sheet)

_____ No known historical sites or gravesites were found on site or would be suspected by a reasonable person to be found on site.
_____ Although historical sites or gravesites were found on or near site, development will not impact.
_____ Historical sites and/or gravesites are located on or adjacent to the site, and will be protected.

Applicant's Signature and Title: _____ Date: _____

Cultural Resources Coordinator Signature: _____ Date: _____

Figure 2.6 *(continued from previous page)* Sample request form for plans amendment

Agricultural & Forestal Districts
Application Packet

This is an application packet for those property owners who desire to add property to an existing Agricultural and Forestal District (A&FD) or to create a new District. A copy of the State law governing A&FD's, as well as, the document that explains the Use-Value Assessment program, commonly described as "Land Use", can be obtained from the Office of Planning. Please not that the A&FD and the Use-Value Assessment program are two separate programs. Information on both of the programs can be obtained from the Office of Planning to assist you in filling out the application.

Please submit this application and the application fee of $300.00 to:

Prince William County
Office of Planning
1 County Complex Court
Prince William, VA 22192-9201

Figure 2.7 Application for modification to agricultural and forestal districts *(continued on next page)*

Application for Modification to the
Agricultural and Forestal Districts
Prince William County

1. Date: _____

2. I (We)

_____ _____

Owner of Record

_____ _____

Address   City   State   Zip   Telephone

Hereby petition the Board of Supervisors of Prince William County, Virginia to [ ] create [ ] modify an Agricultural and Forestal District as described below and shown on the attached maps.

3. Property Location. (Describe concisely the location of the property by distance, in feet or portion of a mile, and direction from the intersection of two public roads or streets.) Example: Located on Rte. 234 (Dumfries Road), 800 feet west of its intersection with Rte. 619 (Joplin Road).

4. Magisterial District within which the proposed district is located: _____

5. Summary of Acreages: (For original applicant only)
   a. Estimated total acreage in proposed district: _____
   b. Acreage owned by persons proposing district: _____
   c. Percent of total acreage in the proposed district owned by persons proposing the district: _____

6. GPIN No: _____

7. [ ] Check if property is currently under Special Land Use Assessment.

8. Current Zoning: _____

9. Briefly describe existing use of the property, e.g., cropland, pasture, forest, type of crops grown or number and type of animals pastured, buildings on property including dwellings and farm buildings, other structures such as silos, etc.

_____ _____

_____ _____

_____ _____

10. State reasons why this application should be supported.

_____ _____

_____ _____

_____ _____

11. I (We) hereby request that the property described above be:

Figure 2.7 *(continued from previous page)* Application for modification to agricultural and forestall districts

[ ] included in the district
[ ] excluded from the district

_____   _____
Name

_____   _____
Legal Address

_____   _____
                                                        Date

_____   _____
Name

_____   _____
Legal Address

_____   _____
                                                        Date

_____   _____
(Signature of owner, or, if owner is not an individual, of all persons required to authorize
encumbrance of this property.)

———

For Office Use Only

File No: _____   Date Accepted: _____
GPIN NO: _____   Acreage: _____
Date referred to Advisory Committee: _____
Date referred to Planning Commission: _____
Date submitted to Board of Supervisors: _____
Final Action: Date: _____
[ ] Approved   [ ] Approved with Modifications   [ ] Denied
[ ] Original Application   [ ] Proposed Modifications
Proposed Period Before First Review _____ years.

Figure 2.7 *(continued from previous page)* Application for modification to agricultural and forestall districts

Chapter 3

Sample Agreements

There are many agreements used in the process of developing land. Some of the agreements are used with local code enforcement. Others are used between a developer and contractors. Agreements used with contractors are covered in Chapter 6. This section pertains more to the types of agreements that you might encounter with local authorities. The samples given here represent some of what you may deal with, but you will have to check with your local authorities for all of the possible agreements that may be needed.

The following forms and agreements will help you prepare for your trek into the world of land development.

Plan Name:_____   Plan Number: _____

Escrow Number: _____

CONSERVATION AGREEMENT

THIS AGREEMENT, made this _____ day of _____, 200 _____ by and between _____ hereinafter called 'Developer,"party of the first part, and the Board of Supervisors of Prince William County, Virginia, hereinafter called 'County,"party of the second part:

WITNESSETH:

WHEREAS, Developer, desires approval of its site development plan, consisting of grading plans (which are part of the approved subdivision or site plans), erosion and sediment control plans, and/or landscaping plans, sewer, water and drainage plans (hereinafter collectively referred to as 'plan'), for a project ('the project') known as _____ _____. Said conservation plan also includes all provisions for conservation measures as required by the Code of Virginia, the Subdivision or Zoning Ordinance, and the Design and Construction Standards Manual; and

WHEREAS, the Developer intends to complete all of the development work contained on the approved subdivision or site plans, including but not limited to roads, sewer systems, water systems, storm water drainage systems, etc., at the project; and

WHEREAS, pursuant to Va. Code § 10.1-560 et seq. and other statutory authority, the County desires to ensure the proper installation, maintenance and adequate performance of such plan during the development process.

NOW, THEREFORE, for and in consideration of the foregoing premises and the following terms and conditions, and further in consideration of the approval of the aforesaid plan by the County and the issuance of a site preparation permit for the work proposed to be done thereunder, the parties hereto agree as follows:

1. Developer has provided guarantee in the amount of $_____ to the COUNTY in the form of one of the following which may be used for the purposes set forth in this Agreement:

    a)   Cash deposit with Prince William County, receipt #_____. The sum dep osited under this Agreement shall be placed in an interest-bearing account and the interest thereon shall accrue, up to a maximum of one year; or

    b)   Letter of Credit # _____ from (Name of Institution)_____.

2. In the event that measures for conservation as provided for in the plan referred to herein, or on any approved revision hereof, are not constructed or installed, the County shall give the Developer notice of violation and an opportunity to comply, and upon failure of the Developer to comply within the time period allowed by the County in its notice, the County shall have the right to enter upon Developer's property and shall construct such measures or do such other work as may be necessary, according to the plan to stabilize and make the site safe.

3. In the event the Director of the Department of Public Works or his designee determines that immediate construction or installation of conservation measures is required during the development process to prevent adverse sedimentation or erosion or to protect the public health, safety or welfare, the County shall give the Developer notice of such determination and an opportunity to construct or install conservation measures within a reasonable time period. Upon failure of the Developer to comply within the time period allowed by the County in its notice, the County shall enter upon Developer's property and construct such measures or do such work as may be necessary.

4. In the event the plan has been installed or constructed according to design, but fails, or inadequately effectuates the conservation measures required by County standards, or inadequately controls sediment or erosion; the Developer agrees to submit a revision to the plan and immediately institute measures to effectuate such measures or control upon notice of such event(s) by the County. In the event Developer fails to do so within the time period allowed by the County in its notice, the County may revise the plan and may enter upon Developer's property to construct the necessary measures.

5. In the event sedimentation and/or erosion from the property adversely affects downstream drainage, any adjacent property owner, or any street, road, highway or other public easement, the County may give the Developer notice of violation and an opportunity to comply, and upon failure of the Developer to comply within the time period allowed by the County in its notice, the County shall have the right to enter upon Developer's property to take such steps as may be necessary to prevent future off-site or on-site sedimentation or erosion, repair or clean up any off-site or on-site damage, or install any appropriate conservation measures.

6. The County shall give the Developer notice in the event tree protection or other conservation measures are not installed, damaged trees are not repaired, dead, dying or hazardous trees or branches within and contiguous to the development areas are not removed, or trees or other conservation measures required by the plan, or required revision, are not installed as specified on the plan, or required revision. If the Developer fails to comply within the time period allowed by the County in its notice, the County shall enter upon the Developer's property to perform such work.

7. In the event County performs work of any nature, including labor, use of equipment, and materials under the provisions of Paragraphs 2, 3, 4, 5 and 6 above, either by use of public forces or by private contract, it shall either (a) use the sum deposited herewith under Paragraph 1(a) and any accrued interest to pay for such work, or (b) draw on the letter of credit provided pursuant to Paragraph 1(b) to pay for such work. The Developer shall be sent notice when such sums are used.

8. In the event any portion of any guarantee provided hereunder is used by the County pursuant to this Agreement, Developer agrees to provide additional or replacement guarantee within ten (10) days of such use in an amount sufficient to restore the guarantee to an amount existing prior to the County's use of such guarantee.

9. It is expressly agreed by all parties hereto that it is the purpose and intent of this Agreement to conserve and protect the land, water, air and other natural resources of the Commonwealth and to ensure the proper construction, installation, maintenance, and performance of conservation measures provided by the plan or revisions thereof, and for the clean-up or repair of all damage on-site and off-site due to failed conservation measures, lack of conservation measures, or to erosion or sedimentation. This Agreement shall not be deemed to create or affect any liability of the County for any failure, lack of installation or damage alleged to result from or be caused by lack of conservation measures or by failed conservation measures, or by erosion or sedimentation.

10. The County shall hold the guarantee until it is satisfied that no further land-disturbing activity will be or is necessary to be ta ken on site in conjunction with the site preparation permit, all required conservation measures have been placed or installed and the County is satisfied that any required clean-up or repairs have been made. When these conditions are met, and in the event the guarantee is not used by the County as part of the cost of completion of development improvements (including required fees), or to restore the balance of

Figure 3.1 Conservation agreement *(continued on next page)*

any other conservation agreement deposit between this Developer and the County to its required level, all guarantee remaining after disbursement, if any, shall be released in writing by the County, through its agent, the Director of Planning.

11.   All notices to be given with respect to this Agreement shall be in writing. Each notice shall be sent by registered or certified mail postage prepaid and return receipt requested, to the party to be notified at the address set forth herein or at such other address as either party may from time to time designate in writing, or by delivery at the site of the permitted activities to the agent or employee of the permittee supervising such activities. Every notice shall be deemed to have been given at the time it shall be deposited in the United States mails in the manner prescribed herein. Nothing contained herein shall be construed to preclude personal service of any notice in the manner prescribed for personal service of a summons or other legal process.

12.   In the event Developer fails to comply with any provision of this Agreement and the County i nitiates legal proceedings to enforce its provisions, the County shall be entitled to receive all foreseeable damages, including, but not limited to, costs of engineering, design, construction, administration court costs and reasonable attorneys fees.

13.   In conjunction with or subsequent to a notice to comply, the County may issue an order requiring that all or part of the land-disturbing activities permitted on the site be stopped until the specified corrective measures have been taken.   Where the alleged noncompliance is causing or is in imminent danger of causing harmful erosion of lands or sediment deposition in waters or imperils the safety and welfare of the citizens of Prince William County within the Commonwealth, such an order may be issued without regard to whether the Developer has been issued a notice to comply. Otherwise, such an order may be issued only after the permittee has failed to comply with such a notice to comply. The order shall be served in the same manner as a notice to comply and shall remain in effect for a period of seven days from the date of service pending application by the County or the permit holder for appropriate relief to the Circuit Court. The order shall be lifted immediately following completion of the corrective action. Nothing in this paragraph shall prevent the County from taking any other action specified by law.

IN WITNESS of all which, the parties hereto have caused this Agreement to be executed on their behalf.

_____

Developer

_____   _____

Federal Tax I.D. or S.S.N.   Street Number

City,   State,   Zip Code

_____   _____

Signature   Signature

_____   _____

Print Name and Title   Print Name, Title, and Phone Number

STATE OF VIRGINIA
COUNTY OF PRINCE WILLIAM

The above agreement was subscribed and confirmed by oath or affirmation before me this _____ day of _____,

200___ in the State of _____. My commission expires: _____

_____

NOTARY PUBLIC

_____

BOARD OF SUPERVISORS OF PRINCE WILLIAM COUNTY

By: _____

Bond Administrator

STATE OF VIRGINIA
COUNTY OF PRINCE WILLIAM

I, _____, a No tary Public in and for the State of Virginia, County of Prince William,

whose commission expires the _____ day of _____, 200 _____, acknowledges that

_____ ,Bond Administrator appeared before me this _____ day of

_____, 200__.

Given under my hand this _____ day of _____, 200_____

_____

NOTARY PUBLIC

Updated 3/3/03

Figure 3.1   *(continued from previous page)* Conservation agreement

FUTURE CONSTRUCTION AGREEMENT
COUNTY ESCROW #_____

This **AGREEMENT** made this _____ day of _____, 200____, by and between _____, herein after called "Developer" party of the first part and the Board of County Supervisors of Prince William County, Virginia, hereinafter called "County," party of the second part.

WITNESSETH:

WHEREAS, Developer desires approval of plans known as (**Plan Name & Plan Number**)_____ _____, and _____ WHEREAS, COUNTY desires to ensure the_____ _____ _____

NOW, THEREFORE, for and in consideration of the foregoing premises and the following terms and conditions, and in further consideration of the approval of the aforesaid plans by the County and the issuance of permits for the work proposed to be done thereunder, the parties hereto agree as follows:

1. Developer has deposited with County, and County by its execution hereof acknowledges that it holds the sum of _____ ($_____) under and subject to the terms of this agreement.

2. It is expressly agreed by all parties and it is the purpose and intent of this agreement to ensure the installation and acceptance of improvements required by the County Code or policies but are not scheduled for installation at this time.

3. Disbursement shall be made only as required in writing by the Director of Planning or his designated Agent for the County. It is expressly agreed that no further consent of Developer to disbursement shall be required by Agent.

In witness of all of which, the parties hereto have caused this agreement to be executed on their behalf.

DEVELOPER

_____

_____
(NOTARY)

BY_____
ITS_____

My Commission Expires _____

BOARD OF COUNTY SUPERVISORS OF PRINCE WILLIAM COUNTY

_____
(NOTARY)

BY_____
Chief, Development Services Division

My Commission Expires _____
FCA 01/00

Figure 3.2 Future construction agreement

County Escrow _____

LANDSCAPE AGREEMENT

THIS AGREEMENT made this _____ day of _____, 200 ___ by and between _____, a _____, party of the first part, hereinafter called DEVELOPER, and the Board of County Supervisors of Prince William County, Virginia, party of the second part, hereinafter called COUNTY, and _____, party of the third part, hereinafter called AGENT.

WITNESSETH:

WHEREAS, DEVELOPER desires approval of plans for

PLAN NAME _____
PLAN NUMBER _____
which plans include the installation of landscaping as required by the Policies and Ordinances of the COUNTY; and

WHEREAS, the COUNTY has determined the cost of said landscaping to be
$_____; and

WHEREAS, the COUNTY desires to ensure the installation and the warranty of such landscaping for a period of one year after the final site inspection;

NOW, THEREFORE, for and in consideration of the foregoing premises the following terms and conditions, and in further consideration of the approval of the aforesaid plans by the COUNTY and issuance of permits for the work proposed to be done thereunder and the parties agree as follows:

1. Developer has provided guarantee to the COUNTY in the form of one of the following:

    a) Cash deposit with Prince William County #_____.

    b) Cash deposit in a FDIC or FSLIC institution in the State of Virginia

        _____   _____
        Name of Institution   Account #

    c) Letter of Credit # _____
        from (Name of Institution)_____

    d) Corporate Surety # _____
        from (Name of Bonding Company)_____

2. In the event measures for landscaping, as provided for on the plans referred to herein, or on any approved revision thereof, are not installed, COUNTY shall have the right to enter upon DEVELOPER'S property and construct such measures or do such other work as may be necessary, provided that COUNTY shall first give notice in writing to DEVELOPER or his superintendent of its intent so to do.

3. If the COUNTY performs work of any nature, including labor, use of equipment, and materials, under the provisions of 2 above, either by force account or contract, AGENT shall disburse to COUNTY on its order within five days of receipt of written demand thereof, such sum or sums as may be supported by invoice attached to such demand. The AGENT'S liability so to disburse shall be limited to the undistributed balance.

4. It is expressly agreed by all parties hereto that it is the purpose of this agreement to ensure the installation, maintenance, and performance of measures provided for on approved plans or revisions thereof, for the landscaping of the property the subject of such plans. This agreement shall not be

Figure 3.3 Landscape agreement *(continued on next page)*

deemed to create or affect any liability of any party hereto for any damage alleged to result from or be caused by erosion or siltation, which is directly dealt with a separate agreement between COUNTY and DEVELOPER.

5. It is expressly agreed by all parties hereto that the amount shall be held by AGENT unless distributed in accordance with 3 above, or paid to COUNTY, as part of the cost of the completion of improvements required by ordinance and/or bond to be installed, or released in writing by COUNTY, the Director of Planning.

IN WITNESS of which the parties have signed and sealed this Agreement.

DEVELOPER - This document shall be signed by an authorized person(s). Individuals who have the authority to bind an organization are partners of a partnership or joint venture, or a president or vice-president of a corporation. For any person signing in a representative capacity (e.g., an attorney-in fact), notarized evidence of authority must be furnished.

_____
Name

_____
Address

_____

_____
Print Name   **Phone Number**

BY _____ its _____
          Signature   **Title**

_____
(Notary Public)   **My Commission Expires** _____

AGENT – The name of the financial institution holding the cash deposit or providing the letter of credit. If cash deposit, then the institution must sign below. If a letter of credit is provided, the institution does not need to execute as the agent. The Prince William Board of County Supervisors is the agent when the cash escrow is posted with the County. Corporate Surety may execute and attach valid Power of Attorney, or attach standard Prince William County performance bond.

_____
Name

_____
Address

_____

_____
Print Name

BY _____ its _____
          Signature   **Title**

_____
(Notary Public)   **My Commission Expires** _____

BOARD OF COUNTY SUPERVISORS OF PRINCE WILLIAM COUNTY, VIRGINIA

BY_____   its   **Bond & Permit Administrator**

_____
(Notary Public)   My Commission Expires _____

LANDSCP1.04/00(updated 2/28/03)

Figure 3.3 *(continued from previous page)* Landscape agreement

AGREEMENT

THIS AGREEMENT made this _____ day of _____, 200_, by and between
_____, party of the
first part, hereinafter called DEVELOPER, and the Board of County Supervisors of Prince
William County, Virginia, party of the second part, hereinafter called BOARD.

WITNESSETH:

IN CONSIDERATION OF the approval by the BOARD through its designee, of a
subdivision plat/site plan/construction plan for a project known as (Name)
_____(Plan No.) _____
DEVELOPER, for himself, and his heirs, personal representatives, assigns, or other successors in
interest, agrees to construct and install all of the physical improvements and facilities shown on
the approved plans and profiles, and approved revisions thereof, within _____, months of
the date hereof.

DEVELOPER FURTHER AGREES:

1. To comply with all the requirements of the Prince William County Code and Prince
William County Design and Construction Standards Manual.

2. To provide and maintain adequate all weather access, including snow removal and ice
control, from all occupied dwellings to a public highway in the primary or secondary highway
system.

3. To be responsible for having the streets and other improvements in any dedicated
right-of-way accepted by the Virginia Department of Transportation into the State system of
highways; to comply with all requirements of the Virginia Department of Transportation for
acceptance, and to make prompt application upon completion of the required work for
acceptance by that Department.

4. That no construction or improvement required hereunder shall be considered complete
until it is accepted by the governmental unit which is to have ultimate responsibility for its
maintenance. The DEVELOPER further agrees to be responsible for all maintenance and
deterioration of the physical improvements and facilities until such acceptance.

5. To provide surety satisfactory to the County in accordance with the County's adopted
bonding policies, to secure performance of this agreement.

6. To indemnify and hold harmless the County from all loss or damage to property, or
injury, or death of any and all persons, or from any suits, claims, liability or demands in
connection with the physical improvements and facilities however caused, arising directly or
indirectly from construction, failure to maintain or use of such improvements prior to final
acceptance.

7. That if any clause or portion of this Agreement is found not to be valid and binding,
the remainder shall continue in full force and effect.

Page 1 of 2 pages

Figure 3.4 Agreement of the terms of approval for plans and specifications for a development
project *(continued on next page)*

This document shall be signed by an authorized person(s). Individuals who have the authority to bind an organization are partners of a partnership or joint venture, or a president or vice-president of a corporation. For any person signing in a representative capacity (e.g., an attorney-in fact), notarized evidence of authority must be furnished.

IN WITNESS of which the parties have signed and sealed this Agreement.

DEVELOPER

Type of Organization: Legal Name and Address:

(EG., Corporation, Partnership, LLC, etc.)

_____

_____

_____

_____

By: _____

                            Name

_____

Title   Phone Number

ACKNOWLEDGMENT OF DEVELOPER

STATE OF _____ :

COUNTY OF _____ : to wit:

    The foregoing instrument was acknowledged before me this _____ day of _____, 200_____, by _____,

(Name of Person Signing Above, and Title, if applicable)

_____.

_____

(Notary Public)   My Commission expires: _____

BOARD OF COUNTY SUPERVISORS OF PRINCE WILLIAM COUNTY, VIRGINIA

                By: _____

                              Chairman

ATTEST:

_____

Clerk to the Board

STATE OF _____ :

COUNTY OF _____ : to wit:

    The foregoing instrument was acknowledged before me this _____ day of _____, 200____, by _____,

and _____, Chairman and Clerk, respectively, of the Board of County Supervisors of Prince William County, Virginia.

_____

(Notary Public)   My Commission expires:_____

Figure 3.4 *(continued from previous page)* Agreement of the terms of approval for plans and specifications for a development project

County Escrow No. _____

SILTATION AND EROSION CONTROL AGREEMENT

THIS AGREEMENT, made this _____ day of _____, 200_____ by and between _____, a_____ corporation, hereafter called "Developer," party of the first part, and the Board of Supervisors of Prince William County, Virginia hereinafter called "County," party of the second part, and _____ hereinafter called "Agent," part of the third part.

WITNESSETH:

WHEREAS, Developer, desires approval of plans for **(Plan Name and Plan Number)** _____, which plans include provision of siltation and erosion control measures as required by the Policies and Ordinances of the County; and

WHEREAS, County desires to ensure the installation, maintenance and adequate performance of such control measures,

NOW, THEREFORE, for and in consideration of the foregoing premises and the following terms and conditions, and in further consideration of the approval of the aforesaid plans by the County and issuance of permits for the work proposed to be done thereunder and parties hereto agree as follows:

1. Developer has deposited with Agent the sum of _____ dollars or secured a Letter of Credit from Agent (No.: _____) in the amount of _____ dollars, and Agent by the execution hereof acknowledges that he holds or has secured such subject to the terms of this agreement.

2. If the parcels covered by the above-referenced plans, or any parcels adjacent to or downstream therefrom, have been cleared, used or maintained in violation of the County or State Erosion Control Regulations, the County shall have the right to enter upon the developer's property or any property adjacent or downstream therefrom and construct such measures or do such other work as may be necessary to prevent further erosion or siltation and to remedy any outstanding violations of County or State Erosion and Sediment Control Regulations provided that the County shall first give notice in writing to the developer or his superintendent of its intent so to do.

3. In the event measures for the control of siltation and/or erosion have been constructed, but fail, through overload and/or inadequate maintenance, to perform the function for which they were intended, County may enter to perform such reconstruction or maintenance as may be necessary to restore performance in accord with the plans, or approved revisions thereof, upon giving notice in writing to Developer or his superintendent of its intent so to do.

4. In the event there occurs siltation and/or erosion from the property covered by the plans referred to herein in sufficient quantity adversely to affect downstream drainage, or travel or any street, road, highway or other public way, then County may take such steps as may be necessary to restore functions to the affected drainage or travelway.

5. In the event County performs work of any nature, including labor, use of equipment, and materials, under the provisions of 2., 3. and 4. above, either by force account or contract, Agent shall disburse to County on its order within five days of receipt of written demand thereof, such sum or sums as may be supported by invoice attached to such demand, provided, however, that Agent's liability so to disburse shall be limited to the undistributed balance in its hands of escrow amount. A copy of such demand and invoice shall be delivered or mailed by County to Developer.

6. In the event Agent makes disbursement pursuant hereto, Developer agrees to deposit within ten (10) days of such disbursement, an amount sufficient to restore escrow amount to its original balance. Failure to make such deposit shall result in the suspension of all building permits on this project.

7. It is expressly agreed by all parties hereto that it is the purpose and intent of this agreement to ensure the installation, maintenance, and performance of measures provided for on approved plans or revisions thereof or as required by County or State Erosion and Sediment Control Regulations, for the control of siltation and erosion, and for the restoration of function of facilities for drainage or vehicular travel if such facilities are adversely affected in their function by siltation or erosion from the property the subject of such plans. This agreement shall not be deemed to create or affect any liability of any party hereto for any damage alleged to result from or be caused by erosion or siltation.

Figure 3.5 Siltation and erosion control agreement *(continued on next page)*

Page two

Plan Name:_____

Plan No.:_____

8. It is expressly agreed by the parties hereto that the escrow amount shall be held by Agent unless distributed in accordance with 5. above, or paid to County as part of the cost of the completion of improvements required by ordinance and/or bond to be installed, or released in writing by County, the Director of Planning.

9. Agent that acknowledges deposit of cash escrow shall be a permanent resident of and shall be bonded in the State of Virginia for an amount in excess of the aforementioned amount of deposit. The permanent mailing address of the Agent shall be included in this Agreement and it is expressly agreed hereto that County shall be notified not less than ten (10) days prior to changing of this address.

DEVELOPER - This document shall be signed by an authorized person(s). Individuals who have the authority to bind an organization are partners of a partnership or joint venture, or a president or vice-president of a corporation. For any person signing in a representative capacity (e.g., an attorney-in fact), notarized evidence of authority must be furnished.

_____
Name

_____
Address

_____

_____   _____
Print Name   **Phone Number**

BY _____ its _____
       Signature   **Title**

_____
(Notary Public)   **My Commission Expires** _____

AGENT – The name of the financial institution holding the cash deposit or providing the letter of credit. If cash deposit, then the institution must sign below. If a letter of credit is provided, the institution does not need to execute as the agent. The Prince William Board of County Supervisors is the agent when the cash escrow is posted with the County.

_____
Name

_____
Address

_____

_____
Print Name

BY _____ its _____
       Signature   **Title**

_____
(Notary Public)   **My Commission Expires**_____

BOARD OF COUNTY SUPERVISORS OF PRINCE WILLIAM COUNTY, VIRGINIA

BY_____ **its**   **Bond & Permit Administrator**

_____
      (Notary Public)   My Commission Expires _____

SILT101/3/00(updated 2/28/03)

Figure 3.5 *(continued from previous page)* Siltation and erosion control agreement

Your Company Name
Your Company Address
Your Company Phone and Fax Numbers

EARLY TERMINATION AND
MUTUAL RELEASE OF CONTRACT

For good and valuable consideration had and received and the mutual promises and releases herein contained, the parties known as _____ (Contractor) and _____ (Customer) do hereby release each other, now and forever, in and from all further promises, liabilities, warranties, requirements, obligations, payments, and performance of the contract dated _____, 19 _____, entitled _____ and made for the purpose of _____ _____ as reflected in said contract between them.

The parties each acknowledge all matters between them regarding the said contract have been satisfactorily adjusted between them, and the contract has been terminated prior to its entire fulfillment and performance, as the parties have agreed such early termination is mutually desirable.

Accordingly, said contract is hereby SUPERSEDED AND ABSOLUTELY TERMINATED.

Each party warrants each's own full power and authority to enter into this Early Termination and Mutual Release of Contract, which shall become effective only upon the signature of both parties.

Date: _____   Date:_____

Customer: _____   Contractor: _____

by: _____ (Seal)   Title: _____

                                      by: _____(Seal)

State of _____ of _____

The foregoing Early Termination and Mutual Release of Contract was sworn to and acknowledged before me by _____ and _____

on _____, 19 _____.

_____
Notary Public

My commission expires:_____   (Notary Seal)

Figure 3.6 Early termination and mutual release of contract

Chapter 4

The Permit Process

The permit process for a land developer can be a long path. The trip is often filled with forms and frustrations. Time can seem to stand still while waiting for permit approvals. But, the day those approvals are issued can be one of the happiest days that a developer can remember. It is a wonderful feeling to hold approved permits in your hands. In fact, you might not be able to contain yourself. After all of the work that goes into a project before a permit is issued, the feeling of posting those permits on the project can be overwhelming.

You learned about the submission of plans in Chapter 2, now you are going to see samples of the types of paperwork required to obtain a specific permit. Until permits are issued, site work does not begin. The day you post your permits is the day that you realize your dream may become a reality.

Types of Permits That May Be Required

Permit Required	Not required	I Already Have It
Clearing		
Demolition		
Road entry		
Land use		
Dredging		
Environmental		
Private septic system		
Private water system		
Street cutting		
Building		
Plumbing		
Heating		
Electrical		
Occupancy		

Checklist 4.1   Types of permits that may be required

✓'What I Need To Do" Checklist

This document is not a Permit   My Permit Application# :_____

General – *Please read the following completely before contacting review agents*

- It is the Applicant's responsibility to active ly pursue all approvals for a Land Use Permits(LUP).
- All releases from required approval agencies must be received at Division of Permits & Compliance(P&C) prior to permit issuance.
- The issued Land Use Permit will be mailed to the Applicant as it appears on Applicant's Address.
- Application(s) will not be forwarded to review agents until the application fee is paid in full.
- **No construction** may begin until the Applicant receives an issued Land Use Permit.
- Permit and plan status inquiries are encouraged on a weekly basis.
- The *Processing Fee* of $_____ is **non refundable**, even if the permit is canceled or denied.
- If you have questions or need help, please call the Permits office. Additional conferences will be arranged at your convenience.

FIRST: After application, **I will** :   [x] post the yellow location marker   [x] mark property lines
                                                   [x] flag corners of proposed structure   [ ] mark proposed driveway entrance

I will also need to provide the following, these documents or actions are **required** to process my application.

☐ Variance &/or Special Exception from the Board of Zoning Appeals. The deadline for the _____ hearing is _____.
☐ Floodplain Management - Please submit _____ sets of complete plans to the Permits office for distribution and review.
☐ Site Development Plans - Please submit _____ sets of complete plans to the Permits office for distribution and review.
☐ Building/Construction Plans - Please submit _____ sets of complete plans to the Permits office for distribution and review
☐ Notify the Permits Office of the qualified ☐electrical ☐plumbing inspection agency **chosen by me** or my agent to perform inspections on the project. *Upon notification, the Permits office will forward a copy of my application to this agency. My agency**may** contact Permits for me.*
☐ Notify the Permits Office of the qualified master ☐electrician ☐plumber, including MD licenses numbers, I have contracted.

NEXT: **In two(2) working days,** i.e._____, **I will contact** by telephone the following agencies marked with a '✓' or 'X' to schedule inspections, field meetings or discuss these agencies requirements(i.e. plan requirements, bonds, etc.). By the aforementioned date, the following agency(ies) are scheduled to have a processed copy of my application making them aware of what I plan to do.

☐ Allegany County Planning Division for street name/structure address at **301-777-3093** (Matt Diaz - Ext 290).
☐ Soil Conservation District at **301-777-1747** for sediment and stormwater management plans (Bernie Connor Ext 109).
☐ ACDPW County Roads Division at **301-777-5955** for driveway inspection/bond submittal.
☐ State Highway Administration for inspections/bond submittal for: ☐ residential driveways at **301-729-8433**.
                                                                       ☐ commercial entrances at **301-729-8465** (J. Wolford).
                                                                       ☐ signs and billboards at **301-729-8451** (M.Murphy).
☐ Maryland Department of the Environment at **301-689-8598** for Waterway Construction Permit (Sean McKewen)
☐ LaVale Zoning Board at **301-724-2285** for zoning questions(*answering service*). *I will need to attend a LaVale Zoning Board hearing. These hearings are generally conducted on the 2nd & 4th Mondays of the month at 7:00 p.m. within the lower LaVale Fire Hall. Sketch plan required*
☐ LaVale Sanitary Commission at **301-729-1638** for ☐sewer and/or ☐water tap
☐ Other_____@_____

NOTE: *The following agencies marked with a '✓' , '●'or ' X' will notify me of actions necessary for permit issuance* .
   Division of Permits and Compliance for Major/Minor Subdivision requirements, review and approval-if necessary.(Dave Dorsey).
   Division of Permits and Compliance for zoning certifications.
   Allegany County Public Utilities Division for ☐sewer and/or ☐water tap (bill will be mailed to Applicant by Utilities Division).
   Al Co Health Dept for (1)well/septic/tap permits,(2)buffers,(3)food service permits, (4)subdivision plats,(5)other requirements.
   Maryland State Fire Marshal Office for review and approval (Hagerstown, MD Office).
   ACDPW Engineering Division for ☐subdivision plats / ☐stormwater management plan review and approval.

MEANWHILE: *If I have questions, I can contact the Permits office for:*

Permit status inquiries or assistance	(301)777-5951 ext. #295
Zoning Certifications	(301)777-5951 ext. #293 or 292
Subdivision Plats	(301)777-5951 ext. #292
Floodplain Management	(301)777-5951 ext. #293
Stormwater and Erosion Control Plans	(301)777-5951 ext. #293
Building Code questions or appeals	(301)777-5951 ext. #352

_____   **Make check**   **Allegany County Tax & Utility Office**
        payable to: County Office Complex
                              701 Kelly Road
                              Cumberland, MD 21502-3401

_____   **Mail permit**   **Division of Permits & Compliance**
        materials, check & County Office Complex Suite 112
        invoice to: 701 Kelly Road
                              Cumberland, MD 21502-3401

_____   **P&C's fax# is: 301-777-5950**   24hrs/7days week

Applicant's Acknowledgment

The following was received and explained:
☐ *'What I Need To Do"* Checklist
☐ yellow location marker(triangular, paper flag)
☐ stakes
☐ Invoice #_____
☐ *Major Site Plan Development Standards*
☐ *Inspection Agencies* List
☐ *Building Code Requirements*
☐

Applicant   Date

\\archive documents\forms\permit_ckecklist._2.doc
rev 8/00   [E3110I] /js

Checklist 4.2   This is a guideline to the type of material that may be needed when submitting an application for a permit.

City of Clearwater
Development Services Department
100 South Myrtle Avenue, Clearwater, FL 33756
Phone (727) 562-4567   Fax (727) 562-4576

Permit Application Checklist

Only complete permit submittals are accepted. Complete application must include the following as applicable to your project:

_____ Permit application form - completed with legal description (Parcel Number).
_____ NOTICE OF COMMENCEMENT – RECORDED – one copy
_____ Plans review fee.
_____ Interior work: 3 sets of signed and sealed drawings.
- Drawings to show entire scope of work – Floor plans, electrical, mechanical, plumbing, structural, elevations, wall sections, details, etc.

_____ Exterior/site work: 8 sets of signed and sealed drawings. (3 sets for Residential)
- Drawings to include items listed above plus drawings showing scope of site work. Engineered site plans shall include parking layout and lot survey.
- Tree survey (including 4" trees and their drip lines on site and within 25' of the adjacent site.
- Landscape plans.

_____ Development Order issued by the Director of Planning, if Flex or Flex Standard was required.
_____ Clearing & Grubbing permit.
_____ Tree permit application or "No Tree" verification form.
_____ Energy calculations as required by State Energy Code (3 sets).
_____ FEMA information for flood zone properties.
  a. New Construction
   1. Proposed elevation of new construction.
   2. Sealed grade elevation survey (NGVD).
   3. Plans shall be signed and sealed by architect or engineer.
  b. Additions and remodels
   1. Need two cost estimates for construction, or signed contract. Building Official may ask for additional estimates.
   2. Photos of existing structure.
   3. Floor plans of existing structures.
   4. Elevation Certificate showing lowest floor elevation (if not on file).
_____ Owner-Builder forms for owner permit following contractor exemption noted in Florida Statute. Must show proof of residency/occupancy.
_____ Asbestos survey for all demolitions & renovations – Pinellas County 464-4422.

NOTE:
Site and building drawings must be submitted together in a package

Permit Application checklist.doc   Revised 3/8/01

Checklist 4.3 This form shows you the type of information required for a permit application.

City of Clearwater
Development Services Department
100 South Myrtle Avenue, Clearwater, FL 33756
Phone (727) 562-4567   Fax (727) 562-4576

PERMIT APPLICATION

PROJECT LOCATION

PARCEL NUMBER _____/_____/_____/_____/_____/_____

PROJECT/JOB NAME _____

PROJECT ADDRESS _____ ZIP _____

BUSINESS NAME _____PHONE_____

LEGAL DESCRIPTION _____

OWNER

NAME (last name, first) _____PHONE _____

ADDRESS _____

CITY _____ STATE _____ ZIP _____

Email: _____

ARCHITECT/ ENGINEER

NAME _____PHONE _____

ADDRESS _____

CITY _____ STATE _____ ZIP _____

STATE REGISTRATION NUMBER _____

Email: _____

CONTRACTOR

CO.NAME _____

LIC. HOLDER _____ PHONE _____

ADDRESS _____FAX # _____

CITY _____ STATE _____ ZIP _____

STATE LICENSE # _____ PCCLB # _____

Email: _____

GENERAL INFORMATION

EXISTING BUILDING USE _____PROPOSED BUILDING USE _____

NUMBER OF STORIES _____BUILDING HEIGHT _____ NUMBER OF UNITS_____

CONSTRUCTION TYPE: I II III IV V VI; P OR U _____

SQUARE FOOTAGE: LIVING _____ COMMERCIAL _____

GARAGE/CARPORT _____ OTHER _____ TOTAL_____

Figure 4.1   Permit application *(continued on next page)*

IF FAX PERMIT, PLEASE ENTER PROPERTY ADDRESS:

_____

PROJECT DESCRIPTION:

_____

_____

NATURE OF WORK (CHECK ALL THAT APPLY)

BUILDING ❑   ELECTRIC ❑   PLUMBING ❑   MECHANICAL ❑   GAS ❑   FIRE ❑   ROOFING ❑

ENGINEERING❑   LAND RESOURCES ❑   LANDSCAPING ❑   TRAFFIC OPERATIONS ❑

UTILITIES ❑   OTHER ❑

TYPE OF WORK: NEW ❑   ADDITION ❑   REMODEL ❑   OTHER ❑   DEMOLITION ❑

VALUATION: $_____

BOARD REVIEW REQUIRED: DRC ❑   CASE # FL OR FLS_____(circle one)   DATE:_____

CDB ❑   DATE: _____   APPROVED ❑   DENIED ❑

• Anyone planning to do excavation work, must notify the one-call "CALL SUNSHINE" Notification Center at 1-800-432-4770 prior to any excavation work being done, in order to prevent underground damage. Federal D.O.T. Regulation Part 192, Sections 192.614 and 192.707.

Application is hereby made to obtain a permit to do the work and installation as indicated. I certify that no work or installation has commenced prior to the issuance of a permit and that all work will be performed to meet the standards of all laws regulating construction in this jurisdiction.

CERTIFICATION
I HAVE COMPLIED WITH ALL THE FEDERAL, STATE AND LOCAL ASBESTOS REGULATIONS CONCERNING NOTIFICATION OF THE PROPER AUTHORITIES OF THE PROPOSED DEMOLITION AND RENOVATION PROJECTS.

WARNING TO OWNER: YOUR FAILURE TO RECORD A NOTICE OF COMMENCEMENT MAY RESULT IN YOUR PAYING TWICE FOR IMPROVEMENTS TO YOUR PROPERTY.
IF YOU INTEND TO OBTAIN FINANCING, CONSULT WITH YOUR LENDER OR ATTORNEY BEFORE RECORDING YOUR NOTICE OF COMMENCEMENT.

I am aware of Florida and Federal Accessibility Codes, and I certify that I have met the requirements of both.

I certify that, this application together with any plans submitted is accurate and represents all work being done at this time. All work will be done in compliance with all applicable laws regulating construction and zoning and if not I realize I am responsible for the removal of any construction in violation of these laws or regulations. Any deviation from information submitted, unless approved by the Building Official will render this permit null and void.

PAYMENT METHOD   CASH   CHECK   ESCROW   CREDIT CARD*   *If paying by credit card include authorization form.

_____
Signature of license holder

_____   _____
Print name   Date

TRANSPORTATION IMPACT FEE (Calculation by the City) _____

Figure 4.1   *(continued from previous page)* Permit application

OFFICE OF PLANNING
PRINCE WILLIAM COUNTY, VIRGINIA

UNDERGROUND UTILITY LINE PERMIT
(Telephone, Electric, Gas, & Cable)

PLEASE DO NOT WRITE ABOVE THIS LINE

Plan Name: _____ Plan No.: _____

Owner/Developer's Name: _____

Utility Company's Name: _____

Utility Company's Address: _____

Telephone No: _____ Address of Site Location: _____
==

Plan Approval Date: _____ Plan Expiration Date: _____

GPIN: _____ Magisterial District: _____

Date Grading/Site Development/Site Preparation Permit Issued: _____

Permission is hereby given to the above utility company insofar as Prince William County has the right and power to grant the same to perform the construction as shown on the approved utility installation plan(s). Said work to be completed in a manner satisfactory to Prince William County by _____ .
(Permit Expiration Date - 12 Months From Date of Issuance)

Prince William County reserves full governmental control over the subject matter of this utility permit. Utilities shall be installed underground in accordance with standards of utility practice for underground construction, and in accordance with standards furnished to and regulations issued by any applicable regulatory authority. Such standards, and any amendments thereto, shall be furnished to the county by the utility company, and shall comport with the guidelines specified in the land use permit manual of the Virginia Department of Transportation, Section 3.200 titles "Guidelines for the Accommodation of the Utility Facilities within the Right-of-Way of Highways". Utility line installation is expected to conform to all the regulations of the Federal Occupational Safety and Health Administration and the Virginia Safety and Health Codes Commission. Should the utility company deviate from the approved plans, without prior approval from Prince William County, this permit shall be considered void and of no effect.

The signatures at the bottom of this permit, indicating approval of the installed erosion control devices by the Watershed Management Division Site Inspector is required before proceeding with land disturbing(construction) activities. This permit shall be considered null and void if this requirement is not met. All erosion control devices, inclusive of dust control, must be satisfactorily maintained until the final release of siltation and erosion control escrow. Mud tracking out of the project site is prohibited.

Application is hereby made for a permit as indicated above and shown on the accompanying plan or sketch. Said work will be done in compliance with the provisions, rules and regulations of the Virginia Department of Transportation, Virginia Erosion Control Law, the Code of Prince William County, the State Corporation Commission of Virginia, the Office of Pipeline Safety of the U.S. Department of Transportation, or the U.S. Department of Labor, so far as said rules are applicable thereto. Upon completion of construction, applicant agrees to maintain all improvements as imposed by the above described entities.

For utility installation in subdivisions where the streets are not yet in the State System, the utility company shall secure approval for access and construction from the developer (Prince William County Design and Construction Standards Manual).

If work is performed in an existing State right-of-way, (road that has been assigned a route number and is maintained by the State), a separate permit is required from the Virginia Department of Transportation. This permit does not authorize construction within privately owned rights-of-way or property .

The owner must notify the Department of Public Works, Watershed Management Division at 703-792-7070 at least 24 hours prior to the start of construction with applicable County ordinances and policies. THIS PERMIT MUST BE KEPT AT THE PROJECT SITE AND SHOWN WHEN REQUESTED.

I have read all statements on this permit, understand the meaning, and hereby agree to abide by the provisions of this permit.

Signature: _____ Date: _____
Utility Company's/Developer's Signature

Figure 4.2 Underground utility line permit application

Permit No.: _____   Receipt No.: _____   Check No.: _____   Permit Fee: _____

OFFICE OF PLANNING
PRINCE WILLIAM COUNTY, VIRGINIA
GRADING and/or GRADING AND INFRASTRUCTURE PERMIT

Plan Name: _____   Plan No.: _____

Owner/Agent: _____

Address: _____

Phone No.: _____   Address of Site: _____

Plan Approval Date: _____   Expiration Date: _____

GPIN: _____   Magisterial District: _____

Bonding Company: _____

Bond Amount: _____   Bond Expiration Date: _____

Siltation Erosion Control Escrow/Letter of Credit #: _____   Amount: _____   Date Posted: _____

Revegetation Escrow/Letter of Credit #: _____   Amount: _____   Date Posted: _____

Application is hereby made for this Grading/and/or Grading and Infrastructure Permit to initiate construction as specified below and shown on the approved plans. Said work will be performed in accordance with the rules and regulations of the County of Prince William and Virginia Department of Transportation. The applicant agrees to maintain all improvements in the manner approved, and in accordance with all applicable agreements, bonds, escrows, and requirements imposed by the County of Prince William and the Commonwealth of Virginia.

The owner/developer understands that this permit authorizes work performed within the boundaries of his property. If access to the property is from a dedicated public right-of-way that has not been accepted into the State System, the applicant must notify the developer who is on bond for the roadway prior to commencement of construction. If access is from any other right-of-way, the owner/developer must obtain permission from the affected parties. Access from State right-of-way will require a separate permit from the Virginia Department of Transportation.

The developer/owner understands that in the case of early grading all grading is done at his own risk. The issuance of this Permit is no guarantee that the final site plan will be approved. Further, per the Design and Construction Standards Manual, active construction of the development under a Site Development/Preparation Permit must be commenced and diligently pursued within six (6) months of the issuance of said permit. Failure to begin such construction within six (6) month period will void the Early Grading and/or Infrastructure Permit. If within this six (6) month period, the site plan has not been approved and the Site Development Preparation Permit not issued, the Early Grading and/or Grading and Infrastructure Permit is void. The land owner shall commence the accordance with the current edition of the Virginia Erosion and Sediment Control handbook, Failure to complete revegetation within the revegetation of the property in accordance with the standards contained in the Design and Construction Standards Manual and in required time period shall authorize the Director to use such escrow funds available to the County to complete such work.

The applicant will assure that appropriate erosion control devices will be installed at the site in accordance with approved plans and in conformance with the requirements of the current Virginia Erosion and Sediment Control handbook prior to commencing actual land disturbance activity. The Department of Public Works will authorize continued land disturbing activities once the erosion control devices are installed and approved in the field. Approval of the erosion control devices will be indicated by the signature of the inspector at the bottom of this permit. This field approval of the erosion control devices is required prior to proceeding with land disturbing construction activities. All erosion control devices, inclusive of dust control, must be satisfactorily maintained until the final release of Siltation and Erosion Control Escrow. Mud tracking out of the project site is prohibited.

Permission is hereby given to the above owner insofar as Prince William County has the right and power to grant the same to perform the construction as shown on the approved plans for clearing, grubbing, grading, and if so depicted, specific infrastructure (storm, water, sanitary). Said work is to be complete in a manner satisfactory to Prince William County by:

_____
(Permit Expiration Date - 6 Months From Date Of Issuance)

If not completed, Prince William County may take action permitted to it under any law or agreements or bonds entered into between the County and the owner or his agent. The County of Prince William reserves full governmental control over the subject matter of this Permit.

THE OWNER MUST NOTIFY THE DEPARTMENT OF PUBLIC WORKS ENVIROMENTAL SERVICES DIVISION, AT 703-792-7070 AT LEAST 24 HOURS PRIOR TO THE START OF CONSTRUCTION IN ACCORDANCE WITH APPLICABLE COUNTY ORDINANCES AND POLICIES. THIS PERMIT MUST BE KEPT ON THE PROJECT SITE AND SHOWN WHEN REQUESTED.

I have read all statements on this permit, understand their meaning and hereby agree to abide by the provisions of this permit.

_____   _____
Owner/Owner's Agent Signature   Date

_____
Print Name and Title

_____   _____
Permit Issued By (Agent for PWC)   Date

_____   _____
Erosion Control Devices Approved By   Date

pc: Department of Public Works/Plan File

Figure 4.3   Grading and infrastructure permit application

Permit No.: _____   Receipt No.: _____

Permit Fee: _____   Check No.: _____

Office of Planning
Prince William County, VA

Land Disturbance Permit

Plan Name: _____ Plan No.: _____

Owner(s): _____

Address of Site Activity: _____

_____

GPIN: _____ Magisterial District: _____

APPLICATION IS HEREBY MADE FOR A LAND DISTURBANCE PERMIT TO INITIATE CONSTRUCTION AS INDICATED ON THE APPROVED PLAN. SAID WORK WILL BE DONE UNDER AND IN ACCORDANCE WITH THE ORDINANCES AND REGULATIONS OF PRINCE WILLIAM COUNTY, SO FAR AS SAID REGULATIONS ARE APPLICABLE THERETO. THE APPLICANT AGREES TO INSTALL AND MAINTAIN ALL EROSION CONTROL DEVICES AT THE SITE, IN ACCORDANCE WITH APPROVED PLANS, BEFORE COMMENCING THE ACTUAL LAND DISTURBANCE ACTIVITY, UNTIL THE DISTURBED AREA IS FULLY STABILIZED IN ACCORDANCE WITH THE REQUIREMENTS OF THE CURRENT VIRGINIA EROSION AND SEDIMENT CONTROL HANDBOOK.

THIS PERMIT IS ISSUED TO ENSURE COMPLIANCE WITH SECTIONS 32-250.50 AND 32-501.00 OF THE PRINCE WILLIAM COUNTY ZONING ORDINANCE AND SECTION 4.08.1(J) OF THE ADMINISTRATIVE PROCEDURES FOR THE MANAGEMENT OF SITE DEVELOPMENT PROJECTS. THIS PERMIT IS REQUIRED FOR ANY LAND DISTURBANCE GREATER THAN 2,500 SQUARE FEET BUT LESS THAN 5,000 SQUARE FEET. IT DOES NOT AUTHORIZE LAND DISTURBANCE GREATER THAN 5,000 SQUARE FEET.

THIS PERMIT WILL REMAIN VALID FOR SIX (6) MONTHS FROM THE DATE OF ISSUANCE. AT SUCH TIME, THE SITE MUST BE PROPERLY STABILIZED OR THE PERMIT RENEWED.

THE OWNER MUST NOTIFY THE DEPARTMENT OF PUBLIC WORKS ENVIRONMENTAL SERVICES DIVISION AT 792-7070 AT LEAST 24 HOURS PRIOR TO THE START OF CONSTRUCTION IN ACCORDANCE WITH APPLICABLE COUNTY ORDINANCES AND POLICIES. THIS PERMIT MUST BE KEPT AT THE PROJECT SITE, DISPLAYED, AND SHOWN UPON REQUEST.

I HAVE READ ALL STATEMENTS ON THIS PERMIT, UNDERSTAND THEIR MEANING, AND HEREBY AGREE TO AIDE BY THE PROVISIONS OF THIS PERMIT.

_____   _____
Owner/Owner Agent Signature   Date

_____
Print Name and Title

_____   _____
Permit Issued By (Agent for PWC)   Date

_____   _____
Erosion Control Devices Approved By   Date

pc: Department of Public Works/Plan File

Figure 4.4 Land disturbance permit application

SIGN PERMIT APPLICATION CHECKLIST

PRINCE WILLIAM COUNTY OFFICE OF PLANNING
MINIMUM SUBMISSION REQUIREMENTS

The following tables list the information necessary to review an application to alter, erect, reface or relocate a sign. The omission of any required items will result in the application not being accepted for review. **This completed checklist must be submitted with each application**.

General Items	Yes	No	N/A
Fees - The application fee for a new sign permit is $44 plus $1.10 per square foot. Reface sign permit application fee is $22 plus $1.00 per square foot. There is a $50 deposit for each temporary sign permit application. Fees and deposits are required upon submission of application. Submit a separate check for each site. (Facade and freestanding sign application fees for the same site may be on the same check.)			
Submit a standard Prince William County Sign Application Form <u>for each sign</u>, completed with all required information.			
For a permanent sign (freestanding or facade), new developments must have an approved site plan and valid building permit prior to submittal of the sign permit application.			
For a temporary sign, an approved site plan is required prior to submittal of the sign permit application (except "Coming Soon" signs).			
Provide a color schematic if colors are regulated by a proffer or SUP condition.			
Submit a building/electrical permit application form with the sign permit application (except when refacing a sign). Application forms are available from the Department of Public Works, Building Permit Office, 792-6925.			

Facade or Wall Signs	Yes	No	N/A
Submit three (3) copies of a sign design drawing, to scale, showing the following:			
• sign dimensions			
• location of the sign on building or unit façade			
• length of building or unit façade			
• projection from building (maximum of 18 inches)			
• type of illumination, if applicable			
• color			
• identify sign lettering (including logo, if applicable)			
Submit one (1) copy of the site plan approved by the County showing facade sign setbacks from all abutting rights-of-way and property lines.			
Submit the following information for any existing facade signs located on the property related to the subject tenant:			
• description			
• dimension and square footage of all facade signs			
• pictures of existing signs			

Figure 4.5 Sign permit application checklist *(continued on next page)*

Freestanding Signs	Yes	No	N/A
Submit three (3) copies of a sign design drawing, to scale, showing the following:			
• sign dimensions			
• height			
• identify sign lettering, including logo, if applicable			
• type of material			
• colors			
• type of illumination, if applicable			
• structural supports/framing plans			
• footing size and footing plans			
• state the design wind speed and loads			
• state the strength of concrete for the footings			
Submit three (3) copies of the site plan approved by the County clearly showing the following:			
• location of the sign			
• setbacks for all abutting rights-of way and property lines			
• location of all easements			
Provide written authorization from the easement holder if the sign is located within an easement.			
Submit a landscape plan showing landscaping at base of sign when located in an HCOD created after February 20, 1996 (see Section 1000 of the DCSM).			
Submit the following information for any existing freestanding signs located on the property:			
• dimension and square footage of all existing freestanding signs			
• site plan drawing showing the location of the existing freestanding sign			
• pictures of the existing freestanding sign			

Figure 4.5 *(continued from previous page)* Sign permit application checklist

COUNTY OF PRINCE WILLIAM
1 County Complex Court, Prince William, Virginia 22192-9201
(703) 792-6830   Metro 631-1703, Ext. 6830   FAX (703) 792-4758

APPLICATION TO ALTER, ERECT, REFACE OR RELOCATE A SIGN

Identify Sign Lettering _____

Site Address _____ GPIN: _____

Development Name _____

Development Type (i.e., shopping center) _____

Type of Use for the sign (i.e., restaurant) _____

Applicant/Contractor's Name _____ Phone # _____

Applicant/Contractor's Address _____

REQUEST:

FREESTANDING SIGN   FACADE SIGN

__ New Freestanding Sign   __ New Front Wall Sign   __ Relocate
__ Alteration   __ New Side Wall Sign   __ Alteration
__ Relocate   __ New Rear Wall Sign   __ Reface
__ Temporary   __ Temporary
__ Reface

Building facade length in feet (wall) _____ Lot frontage in feet (freestanding) _____

Projection from building (wall) _____ Height of sign (freestanding) _____

Sign dimensions in feet _____ Size in square feet _____

Distance from property line in feet _____ Distance from right-of-way in feet _____

__ Externally illuminated   __ Internally illuminated

Is the sign located in a highway corridor overlay district?   __ Yes __ No

Are there any existing signs (freestanding or wall) on the property?   __ Yes __ No

1. The sign permit is null and void should the sign not be erected within six (6) months from the date of issuance, or if any information in this application is found to be false or inaccurate.

2. All sign regulations are subject to interpretation by the Zoning Administrator, and Section 32-250.20 of the Prince William County Zoning Ordinance. (Prince William County is not responsible for any delays in processing this application if the information is found to be inadequate or incomplete.

3. NOTE: A **Sign Permit Application Checklist** must be submitted with each application. Incomplete applications will be returned. Denied applications are nonrefundable.

Applicant/Agent's Name _____ Signature _____
                             (Please Print)   (date)

Address _____ (Phone) _____

FEES _____ + DEPOSIT _____ = TOTAL _____

Log # _____ Received by _____

Figure 4.5 *(continued from previous page)* Sign permit application checklist

SIGN APPLICATION PROCESS

MINIMUM SUBMISSION REQUIREMENTS

1. A permit application must be completed for each sign.

  a. A separate building permit must be secured from the Department of Public Works (Building Permit Office), if required, upon submittal of a sign permit application. Call 792-6925.

  b. A separate electrical permit must be secured from the Department of Public Works, if required, upon submittal of a sign permit application. Call Public Works, Building Permit Office at 792-6925. There are separate fees for electrical and building permits.

  c. Sign permit applications, including the building and electrical permits, will be submitted the Zoning Office.

2. The Zoning Office will conduct a quick courtesy review of the sign permit application at the time of submittal.

  a. A quick courtesy review of the sign permit application does not mean approval, and additional documentation or information may be required.

  b. Sign permit applications must be complete and meet the minimum submission requirements, and should include adequate information at the time of submittal to the Zoning Office.

  c. Incomplete sign permit applications will be returned if they do not meet the following minimum submission requirements.

3. Freestanding Signs: Submit with sign permit application three (3) sign design drawings for each sign, to scale, showing sign dimensions, height, copy type of material, colors and structural supports.

  Submit three (3) site plan drawings for each sign showing setbacks from all abutting rights of ways, property lines, and location of all easements.

4. Facade or Wall Signs: Submit three (3) separate sign design drawings with sign permit application for each sign, to scale, showing dimensions and the location of the sign on building or unit facade, length of building or unit facade and projection from building.

  Submit one (1) site plan drawing for each sign permit application showing facade sign setbacks from all abutting rights-of-way and property lines.

5. The application fee for a new sign permit is $44 plus $1.10 per square foot. Reface sign permit application fee is $22 plus $1.00 per square foot. There is a $50 deposit for each temporary sign permit application. Fees and deposits are required upon submission of application.

6. Sign permit applications will be reviewed in the order submitted.

7. Sign permit applications will be forwarded to the Department of Public Works for final approval after Zoning Office approval.

8. All approved sign permit applications will be available for pick up from the Department of Public Works if they require building or electrical permits.

9. Refacing sign permit applications that do not require a building or electrical permit will be available for pick up from the Zoning Office.

10. If an application is denied, fees will not be refunded.

Figure 4.5 *(continued from previous page)* Sign permit application checklist

PRINCE WILLIAM COUNTY OFFICE OF PLANNING

PLAN NAME: _____

**MINIMUM SUBMISSION REQUIREMENTS CHECKLIST FOR TEMPORARY
MODULAR OR MOBILE SALES OFFICE (DURING CONSTRUCTION)**

MINIMUM SUBMISSION REQUIREMENTS	YES	NO	If no, explain why.
Zoning			
Rezoning Case #			
Address			
GPIN			
Related plan number(s)			
Temp. Sales Office drawn to scale on a copy of the site/subdivision plan (approved or pending). Scale of no less than 1" = 50'.			
Handicap access to temporary sales office. Dimensions of handicap access ramp and/or deck.			
Dimensions, square footage (not to exceed 750 square feet) and height of sales office. Maximum height 1 story.			
Sales office setback from property lines (front, back, side & rear)			
Label centerline of all roads along the site			
Travelways and aisles requires a dustless surface.			
Show travelway width. Must be at least 22' wide.			
Minimum 6 inch compacted 21-A type 1 material will be used for all travelways and parking lot.			
Provide parking lot setback from property lines. Ten (10) foot setback is required.			
Parking spaces (minimum 3 spaces required) with dimensions.			
Handicap space shall be "van accessible".			
Handicap access aisle shall be constructed of 1 ½ inch bituminous concrete or similar hard surface.			
Entrance curb cut location. Provide width of entrance. Entrance to meet VDOT commercial entrance standards.			
Sight distance (minimum 250 feet from both directions) from the entrance to the site is required.			
Temporary sales office must be securely underpinned.			
Erosion and sediment control measures. Provide unit price list for erosion and sediment control escrow (on the plan). Minimum erosion and sediment control escrow is $1000.			
Portable sanitary facilities outside the sales office need to be shown on the plan with handicap access.			

Figure 4.6 Example of minimum submission requirements for a construction trailer or mobile sales office *(continued on next page)*

Show landscaping and provide landscaping detail.			
Standard Prince William County Development Control Form with all information complete (if not signed by the owner, a Power of Attorney must accompany this form).			
Fees in accordance with the Fee Schedule. A certified Prince William County (PWC) review fee calculation sheet.			
ADD THE FOLLOWING NOTES:			
The temporary modular or mobile sales office will be removed within 30 days from the sale or rental of the last lot or unit. The modular or mobile sales office will be removed within one year from the date of approval if all lots or units have not been sold or rented. The office shall be removed within 30 days of the expiration date.			
Hours of operation shall be between 8:00 a.m. and 9:00 p.m.; outdoor lighting meeting the standards of Section 32-250.63 (1) shall be provided for hours of operation after sunset.			
Additional erosion control measures may be added at the request of the field inspector. All erosion and sediment control measures shall conform to the latest edition of the Virginia Erosion and Sediment Control Handbook.			
Developer is to provide accessibility for the disabled as per Virginia Uniform State-Wide Building Code.			
Applicant shall post a notice in one or more prominent locations in the sales office that no sales can be made final until the plat has been recorded for this development.			
No sleeping accommodations shall be provided within the temporary modular or mobile sales office.			
If sanitary and water facilities are not connected to the sales office, bottled water will be provided and sanitary facilities within the sales office (with self-contained chemical toilet) or portable facilities outside the sales office will be pumped out by a licensed pump and haul contractor.			

I HEREBY CERTIFY THAT THE STATED INFORMATION IS INCLUDED IN THE ATTACHED PLAN AND/OR DOCUMENTS.

DATE: _____   _____

                                                           Engineer/Surveyor/Developer Signature

cf:slstrlrchklist1
5/2/02
7/2/02   revised
8/8/02   revised
10/9/02   revised

Figure 4.6 *(continued from previous page)* Example of minimum submission requirements for a construction trailer or mobile sales office

Zoning Ordinance Requirements -Section 32-210.12 (1-13)

Modular or mobile offices may be used during construction of a development for sales and rental activities if the following criteria are met:

1. Such offices shall be subject to approval on an individual basis by the zoning administrator. *[Minor site plan approval]*

2. An approved preliminary subdivision or site plan, which is valid, shall have been issued for the project and final plans accepted in conformance therewith; provided however that for project pending approval and recordation of final plans, the applicant shall post a notice in one or more prominent locations in such offices that no sales can be made until final plans have been approved and recorded and provided further that such office shall be permitted only if final plans are approved within twelve (12) months of approval for such office. *[Checklist item]*

3. The applicant shall submit a sketch of the site identifying the location of the modular or mobile office and construction plans. *[Minor site plan approval]*

4. The modular or mobile office shall be subject to the minimum setbacks of the zoning district in which it is located. *[Checklist item]*

5. The modular office shall be located within the boundary of the project in which lots or units are to be sold or rented. *[Boundary of project is the section or area shown on the final site or subdivision plan that is approved or pending]*

6. No sleeping accommodations shall be provided within the modular or mobile office. *[Checklist item]*

7. A minimum of three (3) parking spaces must be provided. *[Checklist item]*

8. Landscaping shall be provided and the office shall be securely attached and underpinned. *[Checklist item]*

9. Hours of operation shall be between 8:00 a.m. and 9:00 p.m.; outdoor lighting meeting the standards of Subsection 32-250.63(1) shall be provided for hours of operation after sunset. *[Checklist item]*

10. The modular or mobile office shall not exceed one story in height and 750 square feet of floor area. *[Checklist item]*

11. Except for authorization expiring under the provisions of subsection (2) above, the zoning administrator's authorization for the modular or mobile office shall expire upon the sale or rental of the last lot or unit. The office shall be removed within 30 days of the expiration date. *[Checklist item]*

12. Sanitary facilities are subject to approval by the health department. A copy of the health department approval must be submitted with the application. *[Checklist item-note satisfies this requirement]*

13. The appropriate permits must also be obtained from the office of planning. *[Minor site plan approval and land development permit satisfies this requirement]*

Figure 4.6 *(continued from previous page)* Example of minimum submission requirements for a construction trailer or mobile sales office

PRINCE WILLIAM COUNTY
OFFICE OF PLANNING

DEVELOPMENT CONTROL APPLICATION FORM
(please print or type)

FOR OFFICE USE ONLY

Project #: _____
Plan #: _____

1. Plan (Application) Name: _____
2. Engineer/Surveyor: _____
   a. Address: _____
   b. Contact Person #1: _____
   c. Contact Person #2: _____
   Telephone: _____
   Fax No.: _____
   Email: _____
   Email: _____
3. Developer/Purchaser: _____
   a. Address: _____
   b. Contact Person: _____
   Telephone: _____
   Fax No.: _____
   Email: _____
4. Owner: _____
   a. Address: _____
   b. Contact Person: _____
   Telephone: _____
   Fax No.: _____
   Email: _____
5. Brief Description of Application: _____

Parcel GPIN Number(s)	Existing Total Acres	Proposed Development Total Acres	Proposed Development Disturbed Acres	Proposed Total Nonresidential Building Sq. Feet	Proposed Number Nonresidential Lots/Parcel	Proposed Number Residential Lots/Unit	Zoning District	Proposed Use
TOTAL:								

6. Application Includes: [ ] Subdivision Plan   [ ] Plats   [ ] Public Improvement   [ ] Other: _____
   (check all applicable)   [ ] Site Plan   [ ] Floodplain Study   [ ] Chesapeake Bay Study(ies)

7. Magisterial District: _____

8. Waiver Granted :   [ ] Yes;   [ ] No   If Yes, For what DCSM Section: _____

9. Water/Sanitary Facilities: [ ] PWCSA   [ ] Dale Service   [ ] Virginia American Water
   (check all applicable)   [ ] Septic System   [ ] Private Well   [ ] Other: _____

*Signatures: Engineer/Surveyor _____   Developer/Purchaser[1] _____   Owner[1] _____   Date _____
[1] **By signing above, I hereby grant permission to County staff to enter the property.**

*(All Signatures Required – If Owner and Developer are the same, only one signature is needed. Engineer/Surveyor signature needed only if applicable.)   Form Effective: 18-Feb-97, updated 07-Aug-98,01-Jul-03

Figure 4.7 Development control application form

Chapter 5

Environmental and Flood Factors

Environmental elements and flood factors can destroy your development plans. Both of these issues must be given careful consideration before any commitment is made to buy and develop land. State and Federal agencies may be involved in the approval process that you will go through as a developer. This is in addition to local authorities.

Some parcels of land seem fine when you look at them, but there may be hidden dangers. You, or your experts, must make sure that there will be no surprises once you begin the development process. I have seen far too many sites that appeared to be suitable for development and ultimately resulted in cost-prohibitive problems.

Let's look at some examples of what you may be dealing with in environmental and flood factors.

Water Considerations			
Consideration	**Applies**	**Does Not Apply**	**Acceptable Risk**
Pollution			
Flood risk			
Waterways in development area			
Erosion			
Public water availability			
Private well potential			
Public sewer availability			
Private sewage disposal			
Retainage water potential			
Stormwater			

Checklist 5.1 Water considerations

Types of Environmental Risks to Consider				
Risk	Applies	Does Not Apply	Acceptable	Unacceptable
Hazardous waste				
Toxic substances				
Asbestos				
Radon				
Underground storage tanks				
Pesticides				
Wetlands				
General pollutants				

Checklist 5.2 Types of environmental risks to consider

Environmental Considerations			
Consideration	**Applies**	**Does Not Apply**	**Acceptable Risk**
Soil studies			
Water studies			
Pollution studies			
Air quality			
Noise			
Health risks			
Adjoining and adjacent properties			
Traffic studies			
Wildlife studies (any endangered species?)			

Checklist 5.3   Environmental considerations

Characteristics to be Wary of					
Characteristic	**Exists**	**Does Not Exist**	**Is Ruled Out**	**Is A Risk Factor**	**Acceptable Risk**
Stream					
River					
Pond					
Lake					
Ferns					
Cattails					
Wet areas					
Swales					
Erosion					
Culverts					
Retaining walls					
Ridges					
Bedrock					
Potential flood zone or plain					
Visible refuse					
Signs of hazardous dumping					
Vandalism					
Condition of adjacent and adjoining property					
Road noise					
Traffic congestion					
Apparent existing utilities					

Checklist 5.4 Characteristics to be wary of

Prince William County
Flood Hazard Use Permit Application

Property Address: _____ **GPIN:** _____ - _____ - _____

Subdivision: _____ **Section and/or Phase:** _____

Applicant: _____ **Telephone Number:** _____

Purpose of application: _____

_____

I, hereby certify that I have the authority to make the foregoing application, that the information submitted is correct, and that the construction will conform with the regulations in the Design and Construction Standards Manual, any applicable Federal, State, or local statutes, including the Building Code Ordinance, and the Virginia Contractor's Registration Law.

I further certify that the floodplain and/or floodway limits will be clearly demarcated in the vicinity of the construction area and that a copy of the approved permit application and one set of the approved plans shall be maintained at the site during construction.

I also understand that the issuance of an occupancy permit for any structure built within the flood hazard area shall be contingent upon the submission of a Federal Emergency Management Agency Elevation Certificate certified by a professional engineer or land surveyor.

_____   _____   _____
Applicant's Signature   Print Name   Date

☐   1. Application is approved as submitted.

☐   2. Application is approved with the following conditions: _____

_____

_____

☐   3. Application is denied.

_____   _____   _____
Authorized Signature   Title   Date

Planning Office Use:

File Number: _____ Permit Number: _____ Date: _____

WMB.FHUP1   AUGUST 1999

Figure 5.1   Example of a permit application for land in a flood hazard zone

RESPONSIBLE LAND DISTURBER CERTIFICATION
Effective October 15, 2001

Amendments to the Virginia Erosion and Sediment Control Law, Sec. 10.1-563 and 10.1-566 of the Code of Virginia

Revisions to the Virginia Erosion and Sediment Control Law require, as a prerequisite to the approval of an erosion and sediment control plan, that the person responsible for carrying out the plan (owner/developer/permittee) shall provide to the plan approving authority the name of an individual holding a certificate of competence (Virginia Professional Engineer Licenses, Virginia Land Surveyor Licenses, Virginia Landscape Architect Licenses, Virginia Architect Licenses, Combined Administrator Certification, Administrator Certification, Plan Reviewer Certification, Inspector Certification, and Contractor Certification) issued by the Department of Conservation and Recreation (DCR) who will be responsible for carrying out the land disturbing activity. This information must be kept current for the life of the plan. Plans approved prior to October 15, 2001, are not subject to these requirements.

The requirement is applicable to the following plan types:

Lot Grading Plan   Minor Site Plan   Public Improvement Plan   Rough/Early Grading Plan
Stockpile/Borrow Plan   Subdivision Plan   Site Plan

Use this form to provide the required information to the Division of Development Services or Building Development (for a Lot Grading Plan) prior to plan approval and whenever the individual responsible for carrying out the land disturbing activity changes during the life of the approved plan.

OWNER/DEVELOPER/PERMITTEE INFORMATION

PROJECT NAME _____ PROJECT # _____

DISTRICT _____ TAX MAP AND PARCEL # _____

OWNER/
DEVELOPER/PERMITTEE _____ PHONE (___) _____

ADDRESS _____

RESPONSIBLE LAND DISTURBER INFORMATION

CERTIFICATE/
LICENSE HOLDER NAME _____ PHONE (_____) _____

ADDRESS _____

TYPE OF CERTIFICATE _____ CERTIFICATE/LICENSE # _____

APPLICANT/AGENT SIGNATURE _____ DATE _____

DSD Form 2001- 01
September 24, 2001

Figure 5.2 Application form for the division of development services where ground will be disturbed

PLACER COUNTY PLANNING DEPARTMENT   *Reserved for Date Stamp*

AUBURN OFFICE   TAHOE OFFICE
11414 B Avenue   565 W. Lake Blvd./P. O. Box 1909
Auburn, CA 95603   Tahoe City CA 96145
530-886-3000/FAX 530-886-3080   530-581-6280/FAX 530-581-6282
Website: www.placer.ca.gov/planning   E-Mail : planning@placer.ca.gov

ENVIRONMENTAL IMPACT ASSESSMENT QUESTIONNAIRE

Receipt No. _____   Filing Fee: _____

Pursuant to the policy of the Board of Supervisors, the Planning Department cannot accept applications on tax delinquent property or property with existing County Code violations.

SEE FILING INSTRUCTIONS ON LAST PAGE OF THIS APPLICATION FORM

(ALL)   1. Project Name (same as on IPA) _____

PLNG   2. What is the general land use category for the project? (e.g.: residential, commercial, agricultural, or industrial, etc.) _____

PLNG   3. What is the number of units or gross floor area proposed? _____

DPW   4. Are there existing facilities on-site (buildings, wells, septic systems, parking, etc.)? Yes_____ No_____

        If yes, show on site plan and describe: _____

DPW   5. Is adjacent property in common ownership? Yes_____ No_____ Acreage_____

        Assessor's Parcel Numbers _____

PLNG   6. Describe previous land use(s) of site over the last 10 years: _____

GEOLOGY & SOILS

NOTE: *Detailed topographic mapping and preliminary grading plans may be required following review of the information presented below.*

DPW   7. Have you observed any building or soil settlement, landslides, slumps, faults, steep areas, rock falls, mud flows, avalanches or other natural hazards on this property or in the nearby surrounding area? Yes_____ No_____

DPW   8. How many cubic yards of material will be imported? _____ Exported?_____ Describe material sources or disposal sites, transport methods and haul routes: _____
        _____

DPW   9. What is the maximum proposed depth and slope of any excavation? _____
        Fill? _____

DPW   10. Are retaining walls proposed? Yes_____ No_____. If yes, identify location, type, height, etc: _____
        _____

DPW   11. Would there be any blasting during construction? Yes_____ No_____ If yes, explain: _____
        _____

DPW   12. How much of the area is to be disturbed by grading activities? _____

PLNG   13. Would the project result in the direct or indirect discharge of sediment into any lakes or streams?
DEH   Yes_____ No_____ If yes, explain: _____

DPW   14. Are there any known natural economic resources such as sand, gravel, building stone, road base rock, or mineral deposits on the property? Yes_____ No_____ If yes, describe: _____
        _____

Figure 5.3 Typical questionnaire for assessing the environmental impact of a development project *(continued on next page)*

DRAINAGE & HYDROLOGY

NOTE: *Preliminary drainage studies may be required following review of the information presented below.*

DPW   15.   Is there a body of water (lake, pond, stream, canal, etc.) within or on the boundaries of the property?

Yes_____ No_____ If yes, name the body of water here and show location on site plan: _____

_____

DEH   16.   If answer to #15 is yes, would water be diverted from this water body? Yes___ No___

DEH   17.   If yes, does applicant have an appropriative or riparian water right? Yes_____ No_____

DEH   18.   Where is the nearest off-site body of water such as a waterway, river, stream, pond, lake, canal, irrigation ditch, or year-round drainage-way? Include name, if applicable: does applicant have an appropriative or riparian water right? Yes_____ No_____

What percentage of the project site is presently covered by impervious surfaces? _____

After development? _____

DPW   19.   Would any run-off of water from the project enter any off-site canal/stream? Yes_____ No_____

DEH   If answer is yes, identify: _____

DEH   20.   Will there be discharge to surface water of waste waters other than storm water run-off? Yes_____ No_____

If yes, what materials will be present in the discharge? _____

What contaminants will be contained in storm water run-off? _____

DPW   21.   Would the project result in the physical alteration of a body of water? Yes___ No___ If so, how? _____

_____

Will drainage from this project cause or exacerbate any downstream flooding condition? Yes_____ No_____ If yes, explain: _____

DPW   22.   Are any of the areas of the property subject to flooding or inundation? Yes_____ No_____ If yes, accurately identify the location of the 100-year floodplain on the site plan.

DPW   23.   Would the project alter drainage channels or patterns? Yes___ No___ If yes, explain: _____
DEH   _____

VEGETATION AND WILDLIFE

NOTE: *Detailed studies or exhibits such as tree surveys and wetland delineations may be required following review of the information presented below. Such studies or exhibits may also be included with submittal of this questionnaire. (See Filing Instructions #8 and #9 for further details.)*

PLNG   24.   Describe vegetation on the site, including variations throughout the property: _____

_____

PLNG   25.   Estimate how many trees of 6-inches diameter or larger would be removed by the ultimate development of this project as proposed: _____

PLNG   26.   Estimate the percentage of existing trees which would be removed by the project as proposed _____

PLNG   27.   What wildlife species are typically found in the area during each of the seasons? _____

_____

PLNG   28.   Are rare or endangered species of plants or animals (as defined in Section 15380 of the California Environmental Quality Act Guidelines) found in the project area? _____

PLNG   29.   Are any Federally listed threatened or endangered plants, or candidates for listing, present on the project site as proposed? If uncertain, a list is available in the Planning Department: _____

PLNG   30.   Will the project as proposed displace any rare or endangered species (plants/animals)? _____

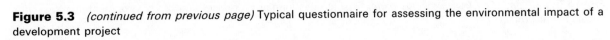

Figure 5.3 *(continued from previous page)* Typical questionnaire for assessing the environmental impact of a development project

PLNG 31. What changes to the existing animal communities' habitat and natural communities will the project cause as proposed? _____

_____

PLNG 32. Is there any rare, natural community (as tracked by the California Department of Fish and Game Natural Diversity Data Base) present on the proposed project? _____

PLNG 33. Do wetlands or stream environment zones occur on the property (i.e., riparian, marsh, vernal pools, etc.)? Yes_____ No_____

PLNG 34. If yes, will wetlands be impacted or affected by development of the property? Yes_____ No_____

PLNG 35. Will a Corps of Engineers wetlands permit be required? Yes_____ No_____

PLNG 36. Is a letter from the U.S. Army Corps of Engineers regarding the wetlands attached? Yes_____ No_____

FIRE PROTECTION

DPW 37. How distant are the nearest fire protection facilities? _____
Describe: _____

DPW 38. What is the nearest emergency source of water for fire protection purposes? _____
Describe the source and location: _____

DPW 39. What additional fire hazard and fire protection service needs would the project create? _____
What facilities are proposed with this project? _____
For single access projects, what is the distance from the project to the nearest through road? _____
Are there off-site access limitations that might limit fire truck accessibility, i.e. steep grades, poor road alignment or surfacing, substandard bridges, etc.? Yes_____ No_____ If yes, describe: _____
_____

NOISE

NOTE: *Project sites near a major source of noise, and projects which will result in increased noise, may require a detailed noise study prior to environmental determination.*

DEH 40. Is the project near a major source of noise? _____ If so, name the source(s): _____
_____

DEH 41. What noise would result from this project - both during and after construction? _____
_____

AIR QUALITY

NOTE: *Specific air quality studies may be required by the Placer County Air Pollution Control District (APCD). It is suggested that applicants with residential projects containing 20 or more units, industrial, or commercial projects contact the APCD before proceeding.*

APCD 42. Are there any sources of air pollution within the vicinity of the project? If so, name the source(s):_____
_____

APCD 43. What are the type and quantity of vehicle and stationary source (e.g. woodstove emissions, etc.) air pollutants which would be created by this project at full buildout? Include short-term (construction) impacts: _____

APCD 44. Are there any sensitive receptors of air pollution located within one quarter mile of the project (e.g. schools, hospitals, etc.)? _____ Will the project generate any toxic/hazardous emissions? _____

APCD 45. What specific mobile/stationary source mitigation measures, if any, are proposed to reduce the air quality impact(s) of the project? Quantify any emission reductions and corresponding beneficial air quality impacts on a local/regional scale. _____

Figure 5.3 *(continued from previous page)* Typical questionnaire for assessing the environmental impact of a development project

APCD 46. Will there be any land clearing of vegetation for this project?_____ How will vegetation be disposed?

_____

WATER

NOTE: *Based upon the type and complexity of the project, a detailed study of domestic water system capacity and/or groundwater impacts may be necessary).*

DPW 47. For what purpose is water presently used onsite? _____

_____

What and where is the existing source? _____

Is it treated water intended for domestic use? _____

What water sources will be used for this project? _____

Domestic:_____ Irrigation: _____

Fire Protection:_____ Other: _____

What is the projected peak water usage of the project? _____

Is the project within a public domestic water system district or service area? _____

If yes, will the public water supplier serve this project? _____

What is the proposed source of domestic water? _____

What is the projected peak water usage of the project? _____

DEH 48. Are there any wells on the site?_____ If so, describe depth, yield, contaminants, etc: _____

Show proposed well sites on the plan accompanying this application.

AESTHETICS

NOTE: *If the project has potential to visually impact an area's scenic quality, elevation drawings, photos or other depictions of the proposed project may be required.*

PLNG 49. Is the proposed project consistent/compatible with adjacent land uses and densities? _____

PLNG 50. Is the proposed project consistent/compatible with adjacent architectural styles? _____

PLNG 51. Would aesthetic features of the project (such as architecture, height, color, etc.) be subject to review?_____
By whom? _____

PLNG 52. Describe signs and lighting associated with the project: _____

PLNG 53. Is landscaping proposed?_____ If so, describe and indicate types and location of plants on a plan.

ARCHAEOLOGY/HISTORY

NOTE: *If the project site is on or near an historical or archaeological site, specific technical studies may be required for environmental determination.*

PLNG 54. What is the nearest historic site, state historic monument, national register district, or archaeological site?

_____

PLNG 55. How far away is it? _____

PLNG 56. Are there any historical, archaeological or culturally significant features on the site (i.e. old foundations, structures, Native American habitation sites, etc.)? _____

SEWAGE

NOTE: *Based upon the type and complexity of the project, a detailed analysis of sewage treatment and disposal alternatives may be necessary to make an environmental determination.*

DEH 57. How is sewage presently disposed of at the site? _____

DEH 58. How much wastewater is presently produced daily?_____

DEH 59. What is the proposed method of sewage disposal?_____

Is there a plan to protect groundwater from wastewater discharges? Yes____ No____ If yes, attach a draft of this plan.

DEH 60. How much wastewater would be produced daily?_____

DEH 61. List all unusual wastewater characteristics of the project, if any. What special treatment processes are necessary for these unusual wastes?_____

Figure 5.3 *(continued from previous page)* Typical questionnaire for assessing the environmental impact of a development project

Will pre-treatment of wastewater be necessary? Yes_____ No_____ If yes, attach a description of pre-treatment processes and monitoring system.

DEH 62. Is the groundwater level during the wettest time of the year less than 8 feet below the surface of the ground within the project area? _____

DEH 63. Is this project located within a sewer district? _____

If so, which district? _____ Can the district serve this project? _____

DEH 64. Is there sewer in the area? _____

DEH 65. What is the distance to the nearest sewer line? _____

HAZARDOUS MATERIALS

Hazardous materials are defined as any material that, because of its quantity, concentration, or physical or chemical characteristics, poses a significant present or potential hazard to human health and safety or to the environment if released into the workplace or the environment. "Hazardous materials" include, but are not limited to, hazardous substances, hazardous waste, and any material which a handler or the administering agency has a reasonable basis for believing that it would be injurious to the health and safety of persons or harmful to the environment if released into the workplace or the environment (including oils, lubricants, and fuels).

DEH 66. Will the proposed project involve the handling, storage or transportation of hazardous materials? Yes_____ No_____

DEH 67. If yes, will it involve the handling, storage, or transportation at any one time of more than 55 gallons, 500 pounds, or 200 cubic feet (at standard temperature and pressure) of a product or formulation containing hazardous materials? Yes_____ No_____

DEH 68. If you answered yes to question #66, do you store any of these materials in underground storage tanks? Yes_____ No_____ If yes, please contact the Environmental Health Division at (916) 889-7335 for an explanation of additional requirements.

SOLID WASTE

DEH 69. What types of solid waste will be produced? _____

How much?_____ How will it be disposed of? _____

PARKS/RECREATION

PLNG 70. How close is the project to the nearest public park or recreation area? _____

Name the area _____

SOCIAL IMPACT

PLNG 71. How many new residents will the project generate? _____

PLNG 72. Will the project displace or require relocation of any residential units? _____

PLNG 73. What changes in character of the neighborhood (surrounding uses such as pastures, farmland, residential) would the project cause? _____

PLNG 74. Would the project create/destroy job opportunities?_____

PLNG 75. Will the proposed development displace any currently productive use? _____

If yes, describe:_____

TRANSPORTATION/CIRCULATION

Note: **Detailed Traffic Studies prepared by a qualified consultant may be required following review of the information presented below.**

DPW 76. Does the proposed project front on a County road or State Highway? Yes_____ No_____

If yes, what is the name of the road? _____

DPW 77. If no, what is the distance to the nearest County road? _____

Name of road?_____

Figure 5.3 *(continued from previous page)* Typical questionnaire for assessing the environmental impact of a development project

DPW 78. Would any non-auto traffic result from the project (trucks, trains, etc.)? Yes_____ No_____

If yes, describe type and volume: _____

DPW 79. What road standards are proposed within the development? _____

Show typical street section(s) on the site plan.

DPW 80. Will new entrances onto County roads be constructed? Yes_____ No_____

If yes, show location on the site plan.

DPW 81. Describe any proposed improvements to County roads and/or State Highways:

_____

_____

DPW 82. How much additional traffic is the project expected to generate? (Indicate average daily traffic (ADT), peak hour volumes, identify peak hours. Use Institute of Transportation Engineers' (ITE) trip generation rates where project specific data is unavailable): _____

_____

DPW 83. Would any form of transit be used for traffic to/from the project site? _____

DPW 84. What are the expected peak hours of traffic to be caused by the development (i.e., Churches: Sundays, 8:00 a.m. to 1:00 p.m.; Offices: Monday through Friday, 8:00 a.m. to 9:00 a.m., and 4:00 p.m. to 6:00 p.m.)? ____

_____

DPW 85. Will project traffic affect an existing traffic signal, major street intersection, or freeway interchange? Yes_____ No_____. If yes, explain: _____

_____

DPW 86. What bikeway, pedestrian, equestrian, or transit facilities are proposed with the project? _____

_____

Name and title (if any) of person completing this Questionnaire:

Signature: _____   Date: _____

Title:_____   Telephone: _____

Figure 5.3 *(continued from previous page)* Typical questionnaire for assessing the environmental impact of a development project

FILING INSTRUCTIONS
ENVIRONMENTAL IMPACT ASSESSMENT QUESTIONNAIRE

Complete the Environmental Impact Assessment Questionnaire and submit 20 copies of this form, one Initial Project Application, the current filing fee, and set of maps. Please submit 20 maps no larger than 8½"x11" (or **folded** to that size), including one reduced. For subdivision proposals, all information required by Section 19.125 of the Subdivision Ordinance for tentative map submittals, must be included in addition to the information listed below. Also provide an **aerial photo** of the site with a scale of 1" = 100' or same scale as the proposed tentative map.

1.   Boundary lines and dimensions of parcel(s).

2.   Existing and proposed structures and their gross floor area in square feet, parking areas with spaces delineated, distance between structures and distance from property lines.

3.   The approximate area of the parcel (in square feet or acres).

4.   Names, locations and widths of all existing traveled ways, including driveways, streets, and rights-of-way on, or adjacent to the property.

5.   Approximate locations and widths of all proposed streets, rights-of-way, driveways, and/or parking areas.

6.   Approximate location and dimensions of all proposed and existing easements, wells, leach lines, seepage pits, or other underground structures.

7.   Approximate location and dimensions of all proposed easements for utilities and drainage.

8.   Approximate location of all creeks, drainage channels, riparian areas, and a general indication of the slope of the land and all trees of significant size.

9.   Accurately plot, label, and show exact location of the base and drip lines of all protected trees (native trees 6" dbh or greater, or multi-trunk trees 10" dbh or greater) within 50 feet of any development activity (i.e. proposed structures, driveways, cuts/fills, underground utilities, etc.) pursuant to Placer County Code, Chapter 36 (Tree Ordinance). Note: A tree survey prepared by an I.S.A. certified arborist may be required. Verify with the Planning Department prior to submittal of this application.

10.   North arrow and approximate scale of drawing.

11.   Vicinity map which shows the location of the subject property in relation to existing County roads and adjacent properties sufficient to identify the property in the field for someone unfamiliar with the area. The distance to the closest intersection of County roads should be shown to the nearest 1/10th of a mile.

12.   Assessor's parcel number, section, township, and range.

13.   Name(s) of property owner(s) and applicant, if any.

14.   An indication of any adjacent lands in the same ownership.

15.   **For areas in the Tahoe Basin only:** Existing impervious surface area (sq. ft.):_____; proposed _____. Impervious surface area allowed (sq. ft.) _____.

FOR INFORMATION REGARDING PROJECTS WITH EFFECTS THAT ARE NORMALLY SIGNIFICANT, REFER TO SECTION 31.450B OF THE PLACER COUNTY ENVIRONMENTAL REVIEW ORDINANCE. APPLICANTS ARE ENCOURAGED TO CONTACT THE STAFF PLANNER ASSIGNED TO THE PROJECT AT THE EARLIEST OPPORTUNITY TO DETERMINE POSSIBLE NEED AND SCOPE OF ADDITIONAL STUDIES.

Figure 5.3 *(continued from previous page)* Typical questionnaire for assessing the environmental impact of a development project

USDA
Form RD 1940-20
(Rev. 6-99)

Position 3

FORM APPROVED
OMB No. 0575-0094

Name of Project

Location

REQUEST FOR ENVIRONMENTAL INFORMATION

Item 1a. Has a Federal, State, or Local Environmental Impact Statement or Analysis been prepared for this project?
☐ Yes ☐ No ☐ Copy attached as EXHIBIT I-A.

1b. If "No." provide the information requested in Instructions as EXHIBIT I.

Item 2. The State Historic Preservation Officer (SHPO) has been provided a detailed project description and has been requested to submit comments to the appropriate Rural Development Office. ☐ Yes ☐ No Date description submitted to SHPO _____

Item 3. Are any of the following land uses or environmental resources either to be affected by the proposal or located within or adjacent to the project site(s)? *(Check appropriate box for every item of the following checklist).*

	Yes	No	Unknown		Yes	No	Unknown
1. Industrial	☐	☐	☐	19. Dunes	☐	☐	☐
2. Commercial	☐	☐	☐	20. Estuary	☐	☐	☐
3. Residential	☐	☐	☐	21. Wetlands	☐	☐	☐
4. Agricultural	☐	☐	☐	22. Floodplain	☐	☐	☐
5. Grazing	☐	☐	☐	23. Wilderness *(designated or proposed under the Wilderness Act)*	☐	☐	☐
6. Mining, Quarrying	☐	☐	☐				
7. Forests	☐	☐	☐	24. Wild or Scenic River *(proposed or designated under the Wild and Scenic Rivers Act)*	☐	☐	☐
8. Recreational	☐	☐	☐				
9. Transportation	☐	☐	☐	25. Historical, Archeological Sites *(Listed on the National Register of Historic Places or which may be eligible for listing)*	☐	☐	☐
10. Parks	☐	☐	☐				
11. Hospital	☐	☐	☐	26. Critical Habitats *(endangered/threatened species)*	☐	☐	☐
12. Schools	☐	☐	☐	27. Wildlife	☐	☐	☐
13. Open spaces	☐	☐	☐	28. Air Quality	☐	☐	☐
14. Aquifer Recharge Area	☐	☐	☐	29. Solid Waste Management	☐	☐	☐
15. Steep Slopes	☐	☐	☐	30. Energy Supplies	☐	☐	☐
16. Wildlife Refuge	☐	☐	☐	31. Natural Landmark *(Listed on National Registry of Natural Landmarks)*	☐	☐	☐
17. Shoreline	☐	☐	☐				
18. Beaches	☐	☐	☐	32. Coastal Barrier Resources System	☐	☐	☐

Item 4. Are any facilities under your ownership, lease, or supervision to be utilized in the accomplishment of this project, either listed or under consideration for listing on the Environmental Protection Agency's List of Violating Facilities? ☐ Yes ☐ No

_____
(Date)

Signed: _____
(Applicant)

_____
(Title)

Figure 5.4 Sample form for requesting environmental information

Chapter 6

Working With Contractors

All developers work with independent contractors. Whether you are dealing with a surveyor, an engineer, or a builder, they probably will not be on your payroll. This makes them contractors with whom you will work. While working with contractors, you will need forms to control them. Written agreements are very important when it comes to arriving at a successful development.

Imagine hiring a site-work contractor without a detailed proposal of what will be done. Will the beautiful trees be cut down? Might they be hit by a bulldozer or loader and scarred for years to come? Will the utility contractor install the sewer main in the right location without a specific, written agreement to follow? How will you deal with changes in your plan? Do you have a change order that will become a part of an existing contract? There is one in this chapter that you can modify and use. This chapter is chock full of dependable forms for you to use as guides when dealing with contractors.

CONTRACTOR RATING SHEET

Job name: _____   Date: _____

Category	Contractor 1	Contractor 2	Contractor 3
Contractor name			
Returns calls			
Licensed			
Insured			
Bonded			
References			
Price			
Experience			
Years in business			
Work quality			
Availability			
Deposit required			
Detailed quote			
Personality			
Punctual			
Gut reaction			

Notes: _____

_____

_____

_____

_____

_____

_____

Figure 6.1   Contractor rating sheet for use in evaluating potential contractors

Your Company Name
Your Company Address
Your Company Phone and Fax Numbers

INDEPENDENT CONTRACTOR ACKNOWLEDGMENT

Undersigned hereby enters into a certain arrangement or affiliation with Your Company Name, as of this date. The Undersigned confirms:

1.   Undersigned is an independent contractor and is not an employee, agent, partner or joint venturer of or with the Company.

2.   Undersigned shall not be entitled to participate in any vacation, medical or other fringe benefit or retirement program of the Company and shall not make claim of entitlement to any such employee program or benefit.

3.   Undersigned shall be solely responsible for the payment of withholding taxes, FICA and other such tax deductions on any earnings or payments made, and the Company shall withhold no such payroll tax deductions from any payments due. The Undersigned agrees to indemnify and reimburse the Company from any claim or assessment by any taxing authority arising from this paragraph.

4.   Undersigned and Company acknowledge that the Undersigned shall not be subject to the provisions of any personnel policy or rules and regulations applicable to employees, as the Undersigned shall fulfill his/her responsibility independent of and without supervisory control by the Company.

Signed under seal this _____ day of _____, 19 __.

_____   _____
Independent Contractor   Company Representative

                                             _____
                              Title

Figure 6.2 Independent contractor acknowledgement

Your Company Name
Your Company Address
Your Company Phone and Fax Numbers

INDEPENDENT CONTRACTOR AGREEMENT

I understand that as an Independent Contractor I am solely responsible for my health, actions, taxes, insurance, transportation, and any other responsibilities that may be involved with the work I will be doing as an Independent Contractor.

I will not hold anyone else responsible for any claims or liabilities that may arise from this work or from any cause related to this work. I waive any rights I have or may have to hold anyone liable for any reason as a result of this work.

_____

Independent Contractor   Date

_____

Witness   Date

Figure 6.3 Independent contractor agreement

Your Company Name
Your Company Address
Your Company Phone and Fax Numbers

LETTER OF ENGAGEMENT

Client: _____

Street: _____

City/State/Zip:
_____

Work phone: _____   Home phone: _____

Services requested:
_____

_____

_____

Fee for services described above: $_____

Payment   to   be   made   as   follows:
_____

_____

By signing this letter of engagement, you indicate your understanding that this engagement letter constitutes a contractual agreement between us for the services set forth. This engagement does not include any services not specifically stated in this letter. Additional services, which you may request, will be subject to separate arrangements, to be set forth in writing.

A representative of _____ has advised us that we should seek legal counsel prior to using information or materials received from _____
_____

We   the   undersigned   hereby   release
_____, its employees, officers, shareholders, and representatives from any liability. We understand that we shall have no rights, claims, or recourse and waive any claims or rights we may have against
_____, its employees, officers, shareholders, and representatives. We further understand that we will pay all costs of collection of any amount due hereunder including reasonable attorney's fees.

_____   _____
Client   Date   Client   Date

_____
Company Representative   Date

Figure 6.4   Letter of engagement

Potential Types of People Needed for a Project

Type of Person	May Need	Definitely Need	Already Have	Don't Need
Real estate attorney				
Lender				
Real estate appraiser				
Insurance company				
Bonding company				
Surveyor				
Engineering firm				
Landscape architect				
Project designer				
Environmental specialists				
Heavy-equipment company for clearing land				
Tree-cutting experts				
Road construction contractor				
Structural architect				
Building contractor				
Sales staff or agent				
Marketing expert				
Advertising agency				

Checklist 6.1   Potential types of people needed for a project

Your Company Name
Your Company Address
Your Company Phone and Fax Numbers

PROPOSAL

Date: _____

Customer name: _____

Address: _____

Phone number: _____

Job location: _____

DESCRIPTION OF WORK

Your Company Name will supply, and or coordinate, all labor and material for the above referenced job as follows: _____

_____

_____

_____

_____

_____

_____

PAYMENT SCHEDULE

Price: _____ dollars ($_____)

Payments to be made as follows: _____

_____

_____

All payments shall be made in full, upon presentation of each completed invoice. If payment is not made according to the terms above, Your Company Name will have the following rights and remedies. Your Company Name may charge a monthly service charge of _____ (_____%) percent, _____ (_____%) percent per year, from the first day default is made. Your Company Name may lien the property where the work has been done. Your Company Name may use all legal methods in the collection of monies owed to it. Your Company Name may seek compensation, at the rate of $_____ per hour, for attempts made to collect unpaid monies.

(Page 1 of 2. Please initial _____.)

Figure 6.5 Proposal *(continued on next page)*

Your Company Name may seek payment for legal fees and other costs of collection, to the full extent the law allows.

If the job is not ready for the service or materials requested, as scheduled, and the delay is not due to Your Company Name's actions, Your Company Name may charge the customer for lost time. This charge will be at a rate of $_____ per hour, per man, including travel time.

If you have any questions or don't understand this proposal, seek professional advice. Upon acceptance, this proposal becomes a binding contract between both parties.

Respectfully submitted,

Your Name
Title

ACCEPTANCE

We the undersigned do hereby agree to, and accept, all the terms and conditions of this proposal. We fully understand the terms and conditions, and hereby consent to enter into this contract.

Your Company Name   Customer

By: _____   _____

Title: _____   Date: _____

Date: _____

Proposal expires in 30 days, if not accepted by all parties.

Figure 6.5   *(continued from previous page)* Proposal

The Masters Group, Inc.

PMB # 300 13 Gurnet Road
Brunswick, Maine 04011
207-729-8357 (Phone)
207-798-5070 (Fax)
tmg1@mfx.net (Email)

PROPOSAL

Date: _____

Customer name: _____

Address: _____

Phone number: _____

Job location: _____

DESCRIPTION OF WORK

The Masters Group, Inc. will supply, and or coordinate, all labor and material for the above referenced job as follows: _____

_____

_____

_____

_____

The following work is the responsibility of the owner or contractors hired by the owner:

_____

_____

WORK SCHEDULE

The Masters Group, Inc. will commence work on, or about, _____.
Work is anticipated to be completed, subject to weather, the work of others, and the availability of materials, by _____.

(Page 1 of 4. Please initial _____.)

Figure 6.6 Proposal *(continued on next page)*

PAYMENT SCHEDULE

Price: _____ dollars ($_____)
or, the price will be based upon a time-and material basis at a labor rate of _____
and the price of materials as stated by The Masters Group, Inc. A deposit will be paid in the
amount of _____ (not to exceed 1/3 of the total price) with additional payments to
be made as follows: _____

_____

All payments shall be made in full, upon presentation of each completed invoice. If payment is
not made according to the terms above, The Masters Group, Inc. may cease work on the project
until all invoices are paid and may lien the property where the work has been done in
accordance with Maine law. The Masters Group, Inc. may use all legal methods in the
collection of monies owed to it.

Should legal action be required, this agreement shall be interpreted under the laws of the State
of Maine. Any dispute, controversy, or claim arising out of or relating to this agreement, or the
breach of this agreement, shall be subject to the jurisdiction of the courts of Cumberland
County, in the State of Maine. The parties hereby designate the venue of Cumberland County,
in the State of Maine, as the forum for the resolution of all disputes, controversies, or claims
arising out of or relating to this agreement, or the breach of this agreement. The Customer
consents to and acknowledges personal jurisdiction over the Customer by such Court and the
Customer agrees to be subject to the personal jurisdiction of the State of Maine.

WARRANTIES

The contractor provides the following express warranty:

_____

_____

_____

In addition to any additional express warranties agreed to by the parties, the contractor warrants
that the work will be free from faulty materials; constructed according to the standards of the
building code applicable for this location; constructed in a skillful manner and fit for habitation.
The warranty rights and remedies set forth in the Maine Uniform Commercial Code apply to
this contract.

(Page 2 of 4. Please initial _____.)

Figure 6.6 *(continued from previous page)* Proposal

RESOLUTION OF DISPUTES

If a dispute arises concerning the provisions of this contract or the performance by the parties, then the parties agree to settle this dispute by jointly paying for one of the following (check only one):

(1) Binding arbitration as regulated by the Maine Uniform Arbitration Act, with the parties agreeing to accept as final the arbitrator's decision (_____);

(2) Nonbinding arbitration, with the parties free to not accept the arbitrator's decision and to seek satisfaction through other means, including a lawsuit (_____);

(3) Mediation, with the parties agreeing to enter into good faith negotiations through a neutral mediator in order to attempt to resolve their differences (_____);

The parties are *not* required to select one of these dispute resolution methods. They are optional. If the parties do *not* select one of these dispute resolution options, check here: _____.

CHANGE ORDERS

Any alteration or deviation from the above contractual specifications that involve extra cost will be executed *only upon the parties entering into a written change order*.

If this contract includes construction of a new residential building or a new addition to an existing residence, it must contain a statement that 10 M.R.S.A. §§ 1411 - 1420 establishes minimum energy efficient building standards for new residential construction, and whether this building or addition will meet or exceed those standards.

If there is any portion of this agreement that the Customer does not understand fully, the Customer is encouraged to seek competent legal counsel prior to executing this contractual agreement.

If the job is not ready for the service or materials requested, as scheduled, and the delay is not due to the actions of The Masters Group, Inc., The Masters Group, Inc. may charge the Customer for lost time. This charge will be at a rate of $_____ per hour, per worker, including travel time.

If you have any questions or don't understand this proposal, seek professional advice. Upon acceptance, this proposal becomes a binding contract between both parties.

Respectfully submitted,

Roger Woodson, President

(Page 3 of 4. Please initial _____.)

Figure 6.6 *(continued from previous page)* Proposal

ACCEPTANCE

We the undersigned do hereby agree to, and accept, all the terms and conditions of this proposal. We fully understand the terms and conditions, and hereby consent to enter into this contract.

The Masters Group, Inc.   Customer

By: _____   _____

Title: _____   Date: _____

Date: _____

                 Proposal expires in 30 days, if not accepted by all parties.

Figure 6.6   *(continued from previous page)* Proposal

The Masters Group, Inc.

PMB # 300 13 Gurnet Road
Brunswick, Maine 04011
207-729-8357 (Phone)
207-798-5070 (Fax)
tmg1@mfx.net (Email)

Change Order

The Contract between the parties shall remain in full force and effect except as specifically amended by this change order.

1. **Parties To This Change Order:**

A. Contractor   The Masters Group, Inc.   207-729-8357
                           PMB # 300 13 Gurnet Rd.
                           Brunswick, Maine 04011

B: Homeowner or Lessee:_____
                           Name   Phone

                           _____
                           Address

2. **Date Original Contract Signed:** _____

3. **Changes in the Work Originally Contracted For:** _____

_____

_____

4. **Price Change:**

A: Original Contract Price: $_____

B: Revised Contract Price: $_____

5. **Acceptance of Change Order:**

Signature: _____
                 Homeowner or Lessee   Date

Signature: _____
                 The Masters Group, Inc.   Date

Each party must receive a copy of this signed contract before work can be started.

Figure 6.7 Change order

Your Company Name
Your Company Address
Your Company Phone and Fax Number

CHANGE ORDER

This change order is an integral part of the contract dated_____, between the customer, _____, and the contractor, _____, for the work to be performed. The job location is _____. The following changes are the only changes to be made. These changes shall now become a part of the original contract and may not be altered again without written authorization from all parties.

Changes to be as follows: _____

_____

_____

_____

_____

_____

_____

These changes will increase / decrease the original contract amount. Payment for theses changes will be made as follows: _____. The amount of change in the contract price will be _____ ($_____). The new total contract price shall be _____ ($_____).

The undersigned parties hereby agree that these are the only changes to be made to the original contract. No verbal agreements will be valid. No further alterations will be allowed without additional written authorization, signed by all parties. This change order constitutes the entire agreement between the parties to alter the original contract.

_____   _____
Customer   Contractor

_____   _____
Date   Date

_____
Customer

_____
Date

Figure 6.8 Change order

The Masters Group, Inc.

PMB # 300 13 Gurnet Road
Brunswick, Maine 04011
207-729-8357 (Phone)
207-798-5070 (Fax)
tmg1@mfx.net (Email)

CERTIFICATE OF COMPLETION AND ACCEPTANCE

Contractor: _____

Customer: _____

Job name: _____

Job location: _____

Job description: _____

_____

Date of completion: _____

Date of final inspection by customer: _____

Date of code compliance inspection and approval: _____

Defects found in material or workmanship: _____

_____

_____

_____

_____

ACKNOWLEDGMENT

Customer acknowledges the completion of all contracted work and accepts all workmanship and materials as being satisfactory. Upon signing this certificate, the customer releases the contractor from any responsibility for additional work, except warranty work. Warranty work will be performed for a period of _____ from the date of completion. Warranty work will include the repair of any material or workmanship defects occurring between now and the end of the warranty period. All existing workmanship and materials are acceptable to the customer and payment will be made, in full, according to the payment schedule in the contract, between the two parties.

_____   _____
Customer   Date   Contractor   Date

Figure 6.9 Certificate of completion and acceptance

Your Company Name
Your Company Address
Your Company Phone and Fax Numbers

SHORT-FORM LIEN WAIVER

Customer name: _____

Customer address: _____

Customer city/state/zip: _____

Customer phone number: _____

Job location: _____

Date: _____

Type of work: _____

Contractor: _____

Contractor address: _____

Subcontractor: _____

Subcontractor address: _____

Description   of   work   completed   to   date:

_____

_____

_____

_____

_____

Payments received to date: _____

Payment received on this date: _____

Total amount paid, including this payment: _____

The contractor/subcontractor signing below acknowledges receipt of all payments stated above. These payments are in compliance with the written contract between the parties above. The contractor/subcontractor signing below hereby states payment for all work done to this date has been paid in full.

The contractor/subcontractor signing below releases and relinquishes any and all rights available to place a mechanic or materialman lien against the subject property for the above described work. All parties agree that all work performed to date has been paid for in full and in compliance with their written contract.

The undersigned contractor/subcontractor releases the general contractor/customer from any liability for nonpayment of material or services extended through this date. The undersigned contractor/subcontractor has read this entire agreement and understands the agreement.

_____
Contractor/Subcontractor　　　　　　　　Date

Figure 6.10　Short-form lien waiver

Your Company Name
Your Company Address
Your Company Phone and Fax Numbers

LONG-FORM LIEN WAIVER

Customer name: _____

Customer address: _____

Customer city/state/zip: _____

Customer phone number: _____

Job location: _____

Date: _____

Type of work: _____

The vendor acknowledges receipt of all payments stated below. These payments are in compliance with the written contract between the vendor and the customer. The vendor hereby states that payment for all work done to this date has been paid in full.

The vendor releases and relinquishes any and all rights available to said vendor to place a mechanic or materialman lien against the subject property for the described work. Both parties agree that all work performed to date has been paid for, in full and in compliance with their written contract.

The undersigned vendor releases the customer and the customer's property from any liability for nonpayment of material or services extended through this date. The undersigned contractor has read this entire agreement and understands the agreement.

Vendor*	Services	Date Paid	Amount Paid
Plumbing Contractor	Rough-in		
Plumbing Contractor	Final		
Electrician	Rough-in		
Electrician	Final		
Supplier	Framing Lumber		

*This list should include all contractors and suppliers. All vendors are listed on the same lien waiver, and sign above their trade name for each service rendered, at the time of payment.

Figure 6.11   Long-form lien waiver

Your Company Name
Your Company Address
Your Company Phone and Fax Numbers

SUBCONTRACTOR QUESTIONNAIRE

Company name: _____

Physical company address: _____

Company mailing address: _____

Company phone number: _____ After-hours phone number: _____

Company president/owner: _____

President/owner address: _____

President/owner phone number: _____ How long has company been in business: ____

Name   of   insurance   company:

_____

Insurance company phone number: _____

Does company have liability insurance: _____

Amount of liability insurance coverage: _____

Does company have worker's comp. insurance? _____

Type of work company is licensed to do: _____

List business or other license numbers: _____

Where are licenses held: _____

If applicable, are all workers licensed? _____

Are there any lawsuits pending against the company? _____

Has the company ever been sued? _____

Does the company use subcontractors? _____

Is   the   company   bonded?

_____

With whom is the company bonded? _____

Has the company had complaints filed against it? _____

Figure 6.12   Subcontractor questionnaire

Your Company Name
Your Company Address
Your Company Phone and Fax Numbers

QUOTE

This agreement, made this _____ day of _____, 19__, shall set forth the whole agreement, in its entirety, by and between Your Company Name, herein called Contractor, and _____, herein called Owners.

Job name: _____

Job location: _____

The Contractor and Owners agree to the following: Contractor shall perform all work as described below and provide all material to complete the work described below. Contractor shall supply all labor and material to complete the work according to the attached plans and specifications. The work shall include the following: _____

_____

_____

_____

_____

SCHEDULE

The work described above shall begin within _____ days of notice from Owners, with an estimated start date of _____. The Contractor shall complete the above work in a professional and expedient manner within _____ days from the start date.

PAYMENT SCHEDULE

Payment shall be made as follows: _____

_____

_____

This agreement, entered into on _____, shall constitute the whole agreement between Contractor and Owners.

_____   _____

Contractor   Date   Owner
Date

_____

Owner   Date

Figure 6.13   Quote

SUBCONTRACTOR LIST

Service	Vendor	Phone	Date

Figure 6.14 Subcontractor list

SUBCONTRACTOR SCHEDULE

Type of Service	Vendor Name	Phone Number	Date Scheduled

Notes/Changes: _____

_____

_____

_____

_____

Figure 6.15 Subcontractor schedule

Work Order

Customer Name	
Address	
Phone Number	
Problem	
Date Scheduled	
Directions	
Notes	

Figure 6.16 Work order

Your Company Name
Your Company Address
Your Company Phone and Fax Numbers

WORK ESTIMATE

Date: _____

Customer name: _____

Customer address: _____

Customer phone number(s): _____

DESCRIPTION OF WORK

Your Company Name will supply all labor and material for the following work:

_____

_____

_____

_____

PAYMENT FOR WORK

Estimated price: _____ ($ _____)
Payable as follows:_____
_____

If you have any questions, please don't hesitate to call. Upon acceptance, a formal contract will be issued.

Respectfully submitted,

Your Name
Title

Figure 6.17   Work estimate

Your Company Name
Your Company Address
Your Company Phone and Fax Numbers

SUBCONTRACTOR AGREEMENT

This agreement, made this _____ day of _____, 19__, shall set forth the whole agreement, in its entirety, between Contractor and Subcontractor.

Contractor: _____, referred to herein as Contractor.

Job location: _____

Subcontractor: _____, referred to herein as Subcontractor.

The Contractor and Subcontractor agree to the following.

SCOPE OF WORK

Subcontractor shall perform all work as described below and provide all material to complete the work described below.

Subcontractor shall supply all labor and material to complete the work according to the attached plans and specifications. These attached plans and specifications have been initialed and signed by all parties. The work shall include, but is not limited to, the following:

_____

_____

_____

_____

_____

_____

_____

_____

_____

COMMENCEMENT AND COMPLETION SCHEDULE

The work described above shall be started within _____ (____) days of verbal notice from Contractor, the projected start date is _____. The Subcontractor shall complete the above work in a professional and expedient manner by no later than _____ (____) days from the start date. Time is of the essence in this contract. No extension of time will be valid without the Contractor's written consent. If Subcontractor does not complete the work in the time allowed, and if the lack of completion is not caused by the Contractor, the Subcontractor will be charged _____ ($_____) dollars per day, for every day work extends beyond the completion date. This charge will be deducted from any payments due to the Subcontractor for work performed.

(Page 1 of 3. Please initial _____.)

Figure 6.18 Subcontractor agreement *(continued on next page)*

CONTRACT SUM

The Contractor shall pay the Subcontractor for the performance of completed work subject to additions and deductions as authorized by this agreement or attached addendum. The contract sum is _____($_____).

PROGRESS PAYMENTS

The Contractor shall pay the Subcontractor installments as detailed below, once an acceptable insurance certificate has been filed by the Subcontractor with the Contractor. Contractor shall pay the Subcontractor as described: _____
_____
_____
_____

All payments are subject to a site inspection and approval of work by the Contractor. Before final payment, the Subcontractor shall submit satisfactory evidence to the Contractor that no lien risk exists on the subject property.

WORKING CONDITIONS

Working hours will be _____ a.m. through _____ p.m., Monday through Friday. Subcontractor is required to clean work debris from the job site on a daily basis and leave the site in a clean and neat condition. Subcontractor shall be responsible for removal and disposal of all debris related to the job description.

CONTRACT ASSIGNMENT

Subcontractor shall not assign this contract or further subcontract the whole of this subcontract, without the written consent of the Contractor.

LAWS, PERMITS, FEES, AND NOTICES

Subcontractor shall be responsible for all required laws, permits, fees, or notices, required to perform the work stated herein.

WORK OF OTHERS

Subcontractor shall be responsible for any damage caused to existing conditions or other contractor's work. This damage will be repaired, and the Subcontractor charged for the expense and supervision of this work. The Subcontractor shall have the opportunity to quote a price for said repairs, but the Contractor is under no obligation to engage the Subcontractor to make said repairs. If a different subcontractor repairs the damage, the Subcontractor may be backcharged for the cost of the repairs. Any repair costs will be deducted from any payments due to the Subcontractor. If no payments are due the Subcontractor, the Subcontractor shall pay the invoiced amount within _____ (_____) days.

WARRANTY

Subcontractor warrants to the Contractor, all work and materials for _____ from the final day of work performed.

(Page 2 of 3. Please initial _____.)

Figure 6.18 *(continued from previous page)* Subcontractor agreement

INDEMNIFICATION

To the fullest extent allowed by law, the Subcontractor shall indemnify and hold harmless the Owner, the Contractor, and all of their agents and employees from and against all claims, damages, losses, and expenses.

This agreement, entered into on _____, 19____, shall constitute the whole agreement between Contractor and Subcontractor.

_____   _____
Contractor   Date   Subcontractor   Date

(Page 3 of 3)

Figure 6.18   *(continued from previous page)* Subcontractor agreement

Your Company Name
Your Company Address
Your Company Phone and Fax Numbers

SUBCONTRACTOR CONTRACT ADDENDUM

This addendum is an integral part of the contract dated _____, between the

Contractor, _____, and

the Customer(s), _____, for the work

being done on real estate commonly known as _____.

The undersigned parties hereby agree to the following:_____

_____

_____

_____

_____

_____

_____

_____

The above constitutes the only additions to the above-mentioned contract, no verbal agreements

or other changes shall be valid unless made in writing and signed by all parties.

_____   _____
Contractors   Date   Customer   Date

                                               _____
                                               Customer   Date

Figure 6.19   Subcontractor contract addendum

Your Company Name
Your Company Address
Your Company Phone and Fax Numbers

CERTIFICATE OF SUBCONTRACTOR
COMPLETION AND ACCEPTANCE

Contractor: _____

Subcontractor: _____

Job name: _____

Job location: _____

Job Description: _____

_____

_____

_____

Date of completion: _____

Date of final inspection by contractor: _____

Date of code compliance inspection and approval: _____

Defects found in material or workmanship: _____

_____

_____

_____

ACKNOWLEDGMENT

Contractor acknowledges the completion of all contracted work and accepts all workmanship and materials as being satisfactory. Upon signing this certificate, the contractor releases the subcontractor from any responsibility for additional work, except warranty work. Warranty work will be performed for a period of _____ from the date of completion. Warranty work will include the repair of any material or workmanship defects occurring between now and the end of the warranty period. All existing workmanship and materials are acceptable to the contractor and payment will be made, in full, according to the payment schedule in the contract, between the two parties.

_____   _____
Contractor   Date   Subcontractor   Date

Figure 6.20 Certificate of subcontractor completion and acceptance

Your Company Name
Your Company Address
Your Company Phone and Fax Numbers

PROMISSORY NOTE

Loan number: _____

Date: _____, 19 _____

_____ (Borrower) agrees and promises to pay to _____ (Lender) the sum of _____ ($_____) for value received, with interest at the annual rate of _____ (_____%) percent payable after _____ (Date).

If this note is in default and is placed for collection, _____ (Borrower) shall pay all reasonable costs of collection and attorneys' fees.

_____   _____
Borrower   Date

_____   _____
Lender   Date

_____   _____
Witness   Date

Figure 6.21 Promissory note

CASH BOND AGREEMENT

BOND NO:	DATE BOND EXECUTED:			
PRINCIPALS(s) Legal name(s)	PLAN NAME: PLAN NO.: AGREEMENT DATE PERFORMANCE DATE: (Agreement Expiration Date) AMOUNT OF BOND (In U. S. Dollars)			
	Million(s)	Thousand(s)	Dollars	Cents

WHEREAS, Principal has executed an Agreement of even date ("Agreement"), requiring installation of all improvements shown on the plat and plans on or before the date identified above; and

WHEREAS, Principal has elected to post a bond, in cash, to secure performance of the terms and conditions of the said Agreement,

NOW, THEREFORE, _____ as Principal of said Agreement and this Bond and the Board of County Supervisors of Prince William County, Virginia (hereinafter called County), as Obligee, hereby agreed as follows:

1. The County acknowledges receipt of the Bond amount, _____
_____($_____), to be invested, held and applied in accordance with the terms of this Bond Agreement.

2. The condition of this Bond is that Principal is held and firmly bound to the County in the sum written above in lawful money of the United States of America, as security for Principal's performance of the Agreement identified above.

3. County shall deposit said sum in an interest-bearing account in an institution insured by FDIC or FSLIC for the term of the Performance Agreement and any approved extensions thereof, provided that the principal sum may be reduced and refunded to Principal in accordance with adopted bond reduction policies.

4. If the Principal defaults in the performance of all or any part of the obligations of the Agreement or abandons the work, the Director of the Office of Planning shall give written notice of same to Principal, specifying the principle items of breach. Notice expressly given under paragraph 4 shall terminate whatever rights Principal may have to perform further work under the Agreement.

5. In the event of default by the Principal as defined in paragraph 4 above, the County shall apply the Cash Bond and any accrued interest to completion of work required by the Agreement. Any funds remaining after completion shall be returned to Principal. If the Cash Bond funds are not sufficient to complete the work, County may recover the deficiency from the Principal.

Figure 6.22 Cash bond agreement *(continued on next page)*

Bond No. _____

6. Computation of damages attributable to Principal's breach and chargeable against the Bond shall include not only the direct costs of completion, but also procurement costs, litigation costs, to include reasonable attorney's fees, administrative costs, expenses due to delay caused by Principal, maintenance and repair costs, and inspection fees.

7. Any notice required hereunder shall be deemed effective if given by registered mail, return receipt requested, to Principal in the name and at the address given in accordance with this paragraph. Any notice to the County shall be so given to the Director of Planning, 1 County Complex Court, Prince William, Virginia 22192 or subsequent address notice of which is given as provided herein.

Figure 6.22 *(continued from previous page)* Cash bond agreement

Bond No. _____

WITNESS the following signatures and seals:

PRINCIPAL

This document shall be signed by an authorized person(s). Individuals who have the authority to bind an organization are partners of a partnership or joint venture, or a president or vice-president of a corporation. For any person signing in a representative capacity (e.g., an attorney-in fact), notarized evidence of authority must be furnished.

Type of Organization: Legal Name and Address:

_____   _____ (SEAL)

State of Incorporation: _____

_____   _____

                                                     _____

Federal Tax I.D. or S.S.N.

                                        Signature(s):

_____

                                        BY: _____
                                                         Name

                                        _____
                                                         Title

ACKNOWLEDGMENT OF PRINCIPAL

STATE OF _____:

COUNTY OF _____, to wit:

        The foregoing instrument was acknowledged before me this _____ day of

_____, 19_____, by _____
                                             (Name of person signing above and title)

_____
            Notary Public   My Commission expires_____

Figure 6.22 *(continued from previous page)* Cash bond agreement

BOARD OF COUNTY SUPERVISORS OF PRINCE WILLIAM COUNTY, VIRGINIA

By: _____
                    Chairman

ATTEST:

_____
            Clerk to the Board

STATE OF VIRGINIA

COUNTY OF PRINCE WILLIAM, to wit:

    The foregoing instrument was acknowledged before me this _____ day of

_____, 200_____, by _____ and

_____, Chairman and Clerk, respectively, of the

Board of County Supervisors of Prince William County, Virginia.

_____   _____
        Notary Public   My commission expires _____

Figure 6.22 *(continued from previous page)* Cash bond agreement

PERFORMANCE BOND

BOND NO:	DATE BOND EXECUTED:			
PRINCIPALS(s) Legal name(s) . **SURETY(IES)**	**PLAN NAME**: **PLAN NO.**: **AGREEMENT DATE**: **PERFORMANCE DATE**: (Agreement Expiration Date) **AMOUNT OF BOND** (IN U.S. DOLLARS)			
	Million(s)	Thousand(s)	Dollar(s)	Cents

KNOW ALL MEN BY THESE PRESENTS, that we, the Principal and Surety hereto recite and declare that:

    1. We are held and firmly bound to the obligee Board of County Supervisors of Prince William County, Virginia (hereinafter called County), in the sum written above in lawful money of the United States of America, to be paid to the County, its successors or assigns, for the payment whereof Principal and Surety bind themselves, their heirs, executors, administrators, successors, and assigns, jointly and severally, firmly by this Bond.

    2. The condition of this Bond is that if the Principal shall in every respect perform all of its obligations under the Agreement identified above, which Agreement is incorporated herein by reference, then this Bond shall be void; otherwise, the Bond shall continuously remain in full force and effect until discharge in accordance with its terms.

    3. (a) Surety expressly waives any right to receive notice, review or approve any revisions to the plans, profiles and specifications referred to in the Agreement. No such revision or alteration in the work required to meet County or State standards shall in any way affect the obligation of the Surety under this Bond.

    (b) By signature hereto, the Surety consents to any extension of time granted to the Principal, to permit performance of the obligations of the Agreement this Bond secures, whether or not Surety receives notice of same, provided such additional period shall not exceed the original period allowed for performance in the Agreement without notice to and consent by the Surety.

    4. Default shall be deemed to have occurred on the part of the Principal if Principal shall fail to complete its obligations under the Agreement within the time set forth therein or any extensions thereof; and default shall be deemed to have occurred prior to the expiration of such period if, in the judgment of the Director of Planning (Director), the Principal has:

    (a) abandoned the performance of its obligations under the Agreement; or,

Figure 6.23   Performance bond *(continued on next page)*

(b) renounced or repudiated its obligations under the Agreement; or

(c) Clearly demonstrated through insolvency, or otherwise, that its obligations under the Agreement cannot be completed within the time allotted under the Agreement.

5. In the event of default by the Principal, as defined in paragraph 4 of this Bond, the Director shall give written notice of such default to the Principal and Surety. In such event, the Surety shall elect either of the following options:

(a) Within 30 days of receipt of the default notice, Surety shall pay over to the County the full face value sum of the Bond or such lesser amount as may be specified by the Director, in his sole discretion, and be relieved of further liability under this Bond. If this option is selected by Surety, the County will take over or relet all or any part of the work required by the Agreement but not completed, and will complete the same to the extent of available funds. The costs and expenses of completing the work shall include all items set forth in Paragraph 6(b) of this Bond. If Bond funds are not sufficient to complete the work, then the County may proceed against the Principal for any difference. If there are any funds left which are not necessary for completion of the work, the County will return this excess to Surety within 30 days after work is completed; or,

(b) Within 30 days of receipt of the default notice, Surety shall give written notice to the County that it will assume the Agreement and the obligations of the Principal and shall complete the Agreement according to its terms and provisions within 180 days of said notice, the time remaining under the Performance Agreement, or such other term as may be approved by Director. In the event that Surety elects this option and then fails to faithfully perform all or any part of the work or should it unnecessarily delay all or any part of the work, then the County may proceed as provided in Paragraph 6 of this Bond.

6. Should Surety fail to elect either option in Paragraph 5 above within 30 days of receipt of default notice, or having elected option (b), should thereafter fail to perform, then in either event the County may elect among the procedures set forth in this paragraph, in any combination. The County may:

(a) take over or relet all or any part of the work not completed and complete the same for the account and at the expense of the Principal and Surety, who shall be jointly and severally liable to the County for the costs incurred in completion, including all items set forth in Paragraph 6(b) of this Bond as the measure of damages; the actual cost to obligee, as evidenced by the written statement of the Director, shall be conclusive upon Principal and Surety as to the quantum of damages; or

(b) bring suit, action or proceedings to enforce the provisions of this Bond. In such event, it is expressly agreed and understood that, regardless of the date of breach of the underlying Agreement or of the obligations of this Bond, the measure of damages recoverable shall be the cost of completion and/or correction of the work required by the Agreement as of the earliest of the following three dates:

(a) when the work is actually completed and/or corrected to local and state approval and acceptance;

Figure 6.23   *(continued from previous page)* Performance bond

Bond No. _____

(b) final judgment of a court of competent jurisdiction;

(c) two years from the expiration of the underlying Agreement or last extension thereof.

It is further expressly agreed and understood that the measure of damages shall include in addition to the direct cost of completion or repair, expenses attributable to litigation costs, attorney's fees, procurement costs, and any cost increases arising from delay occasioned by litigation, or other proceedings necessary to enforce the provisions of this Bond, and by delays by Surety under paragraph 5(b) of this Bond.

7. In any action or proceeding initiated in connection with this Bond, and any and all obligations arising hereunder, the venue shall be the County of Prince William, Commonwealth of Virginia.

8. If any one or more of the provisions of this Bond are determined to be illegal or unenforceable by the court of competent jurisdiction, all other provisions shall remain effective.

9. Whenever notice is required, it shall be deemed given if mailed registered, return receipt requested, in the names and to the addresses given below; provided, however, that notice of change of address shall be effective if given in accordance with this paragraph. Any notice to the County shall be so given to the Director of Planning, 1 County Complex Court, Prince William Virginia 22192 or subsequent address notice of which is given as provided herein.

IN WITNESS WHEREOF, the parties hereto have caused this Bond Agreement to be executed as of the day and year set forth above.

Figure 6.23 *(continued from previous page)* Performance bond

Bond No. _____

PRINCIPAL

Type of Organization: Legal Name and Address:
"(e.g., Corporation, Partnership, Limited Liability
    Company, etc.)"
_____   _____ (SEAL)

State of Incorporation: _____

_____   _____

                                                _____

                                                Signature(s):

                                                BY: _____
                                                              Name

                                                _____
                                                         Title   Phone #

ACKNOWLEDGMENT OF PRINCIPAL

STATE OF _____:

COUNTY OF _____, to wit:

        The foregoing instrument was acknowledged before me this _____ day of

_____, 19_____, by _____
                                          (name of person signing above and title)

_____   My commission expires _____
         Notary Public

Figure 6.23   *(continued from previous page)* Performance bond

Bond No. _____

CORPORATE SURETY

State of Incorporation: Legal Name and Address:

_____   _____ (SEAL)

                           _____

                           _____

                           _____

Signature(s):

BY: _____

                            Name

              _____

                            Title

ACKNOWLEDGMENT OF CORPORATE SURETY

STATE OF _____ :

COUNTY OF _____ , to wit:

     The foregoing instrument was acknowledged before me this _____ day of

_____ , 19_____ , by _____

                            (name of person signing above and title)

_____

     Notary Public   My commission expires _____

                                Attach valid Power of Attorney

Figure 6.23   *(continued from previous page)* Performance bond

USDA
Form RD 1924-12
(Rev. 1-00)

INSPECTION REPORT

FORM APPROVED
OMB No. 0575-0042

STATE _____

FOR _____ COUNTY_____

ADDRESS _____

ITEM OF DEVELOPMENT	PERCENT COMPLETE	ITEM OF DEVELOPMENT	PERCENT COMPLETE

PERIODIC INSPECTION

Date & No. of previous inspection: _____

This inspection is Number _____

ITEMIZE AND DESCRIBE the significant conditions observed to be at variance with the approved plans and specifications and make your recommendations for correcting the deficiencies. Also make comments with respect to the progress of the work. In the case of development performed by the borrower method, carefully compare work accomplished with funds available and record any facts which indicate that actual costs are significantly at variance with planned costs. Check to see that deficiencies previously reported have been corrected.

_____
_____
_____
_____
_____
_____

(See attached sheets for additional comments)

DATE _____ SIGNED _____

Indicate whether: ☐ *Agency Representative, or*
  ☐ *Contractor*

FINAL INSPECTION

I CERTIFY that I have inspected for the purposes set forth in 7 C.F.R. 1924 subpart A and 7 C.F.R. 1942 subpart A, the above listed items of development and that those shown as 100% complete have been completed in accordance with the Drawings and Specifications or other descriptive material. Health Department approval has been given the water and waste disposal system

on (date) _____ Builder's Warranty is dated _____

DATE _____ SIGNED _____
  USDA Representative

The undersigned gives approval of acceptance of the work constructed under the conditions of the contract and Builder's Warranty.

DATE _____ SIGNED _____
  Borrower

DATE _____ SIGNED _____
  Builder (Optional)

According to the Paperwork Reduction Act of 1995, no persons are required to respond to a collection of information unless it displays a valid OMB control number. The valid OMB control number for this information collection is 0575-0042. The time required to complete this information collection is estimated to average 15 minutes per response, including the time for reviewing instructions, searching existing data sources, gathering and maintaining the data needed, and completing and reviewing the collection of information.

POSITION 6

Figure 6.24 Inspection report *(continued on next page)*

GUIDE FOR INSPECTION OF CONSTRUCTION OF
DWELLINGS AND BUILDINGS

Notices, Labor and Occupancy Observations.

☐ Yes ☐ NO - The required posters displayed?

☐ Yes ☐ NO - The facilities segregated?

☐ Yes ☐ NO - Amy evidence of employment discrimination?

GENERAL. - Drainage conditions. Location of buildings with respect to property lines: Other buildings, water supply, sewage disposal, utilities, etc. Protection of materials on site.

EXCAVATION. - Earth bearing. Footing depths. Frost lines. Grades specified.

CONCRETE AND MASONRY. - Concrete mix or strength, forms, placing. Mortar mix. Width and depth of footings. Reinforcing steel. Stepped footings. Drain title. Concrete slabs on ground: Bed under slabs, wire mesh, slab thickness, finish. Termite protection. Foundation wall and pier alignment. Anchorage preparation. Dampproofing. Waterproofing. Exterior masonry: Lintels, wall thickness, height, parging, furring, wall vents, basement windows, termite protection, Masonry veneer: Lintels, thickness, airspace, flashing, felt, bonding, weepholes. Interior masonry wall: Thickness, lintels. All masonry walls: Joints, tooling, pointing, flashing, prevention of mortar stains, cleaning, Masonry chimney and fireplaces: Flues, size of flues, height above ridge, thimble, chimney cap, smoke cap, smoke chambers, firebrick, hearth. Basementless areas: Clearance below joist, positive drainage.

CARPENTRY MATERIALS. - Species and grade of lumber, moisture content. Shims. Preservatives.

FRAMING. - Fire stopping. Framing at chimney. Columns. Posts. Anchorage and moisture protection. Girders. Floor joists, double joists. Headers and trimmers. Subflooring. Ceiling joists. Roof pitch. Roof rafters. Hip and valley rafters. Collar beams. Flat roofs. Trussed roof construction. Studs, corner construction, corner bracing. Sill construction. Anchorage. Window and door openings. Plates. Wall sheathing. Roof sheathing. Termite protection.

EXTERIOR WALL FINISH. -Type of paper or felt. Lap. Fit at: Comer boards, door and window casings, drip cap, water table, sills, Nails and nailing. Miter. Comer finish. Stucco.

ROOF COVERING. - Conditions of deck, underlay, starting course, exposure, nailing.

INSULATION. - Fastening of boards. Fill (to top of walls and even distribution in ceilings).

FLASHING AND CAULKING. - Flashing at: exterior heads of openings, chimneys, intersections of roof and walls, valleys, hips, ridges. Caulking around openings

PLUMBING. - Quality of materials Workmanship. Excavation and backfill. Protection of pipes. Size of pipe. Cutting or notching. Joints and connections. Water supply lines: On solid ground below frost, shut- off valve, drain valve for entire system. Drainage system, vents and venting. Traps and clean outs. Hangers and supports. Quality and type of fixtures. Location of fixtures. Fixtures securely installed. Domestic hot water heating and storage, equipment, safety, capacity.

HEATING. - Safety, capacity. Required tests, operating and maintenance instruction. Fuel storage. Check operation.

GAS (Liquefied Petroleum). - Approval markings on tank. Tank Location. Meter installation (hung properly). Protection of exposed pipe. Leakage under pressure (smell joints). Location of shut-off valve inside building. Proper ventilation of system.

ELECTRICAL. - Location of meter. Number of circuits. Provision for future circuits. Location of outlets and switches. Power suppliers approval.

DRYWALL. - Joints, sanding, filling, taping.

GLAZING. - Quality of glass, putty, application.

LATHING AND PLASTERING. - Quality of lath, evenness, grounds, joints between work and masonry, finishing.

MISCELLANEOUS METALWORK. - Pipe rail, metal bucks, metal windows (setting, caulking and priming), painting.

MILLWORK. - Trim, cabinets, windows and doors, thresholds.

WEATHER STRIPPING. - Seal, joints (tight and smooth).

FINISH FLOORS. - Dry storage, baseboard clearance, joints, nailing, finish, protection after laying.

SCREENING. - Screen cloth, tightness, fit, operation, identification tags, paint splashes.

HARDWARE. - Materials, workmanship, operation, keys.

LIGHTING FIXTURES. - Type, bulbs (light, clean).

PAINTING AND DECORATING. - Surface preparation, washable materials, lead content, application (suitable weather), nail heads.

BACKFILLING. - Around masonry, around trees. Finish grade 8 inches below wood.

LANDSCAPING. - Planting, seeding, finish grades.

FINAL. - Cleaning up: Masonry, crawl and pipe space, pipe chases, attic, vents in walls, floors, chimney bottoms, fireplace throat, glass, hardware and fixtures. Removal of debris. Closing of floor openings around pipes. Replacement of broken windows. Operation of doors and windows.

WATER SUPPLY

Location with respect to possible sources of contamination. Shaft. Protection from contamination. Construction. Watertight casing safe distance above slab and safe distance below ground surface. Grading at top of well to drain away in all directions. Size of concrete platform. Slope of concrete platform. Pump: Type, capacity, location, protection, pollution proof, frost proof. Capacity of pressure tank.

SEWAGE DISPOSAL

Location: Slope of grade, depth of ground water, existing and future water supply. Size and slope of house sewer to septic tank. Capacity of tank. Distance of tank from foundation wall. Construction of tank, Location of disposal field (unobstructed and unshaded area). Construction of field. Minimum seepage area (determined by percolation test or recommendation of Soil Conservation Service and State Board of Health). Approval of State Board of Health.

RD 1924-12
REVERSE

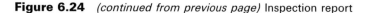

Figure 6.24 *(continued from previous page)* Inspection report

BID BOND *(See instruction on reverse)*	DATE BOND EXECUTED *(Must not be later than bid opening date)*	OMB NO.: **9000-0045**

Public reporting burden for this collection of information is estimated to average 25 minutes per response, including the time for reviewing instructions, searching existing data sources, gathering and maintaining the data needed, and completing and reviewing the collection of information. Send comments regarding this burden estimate or any other aspect of this collection of information, including suggestions for reducing this burden, to the FAR Secretariat (MVR), Federal Acquisition Policy Division, GSA, Washington, DC 20405.

PRINCIPAL *(Legal name and business address)*

TYPE OF ORGANIZATION *("X" one)*

☐ INDIVIDUAL ☐ PARTNERSHIP

☐ JOINT VENTURE ☐ CORPORATION

STATE OF INCORPORATION

SURETY(IES) *(Name and business address)*

PENAL SUM OF BOND					BID IDENTIFICATION	
PERCENT OF BID PRICE	AMOUNT NOT TO EXCEED				BID DATE	INVITATION NO.
	MILLION(S)	THOUSAND(S)	HUNDRED(S)	CENTS		
					FOR *(Construction, Supplies, or Services)*	

OBLIGATION:

We, the Principal and Surety(ies) are firmly bound to the United States of America (hereinafter called the Government) in the above penal sum. For payment of the penal sum, we bind ourselves, our heirs, executors, administrators, and successors, jointly and severally. However, where the Sureties are corporations acting as co-sureties, we, the Sureties, bind ourselves in such sum "jointly and severally" as well as "severally" only for the purpose of allowing a joint action or actions against any or all of us. For all other purposes, each Surety binds itself, jointly and severally with the Principal, for the payment of the sum shown opposite the name of the Surety. If no limit of liability is indicated, the limit of liability is the full amount of the penal sum.

CONDITIONS:

The Principal has submitted the bid identified above.

THEREFORE:

The above obligation is void if the Principal - (a) upon acceptance by the Government of the bid identified above, within the period specified therein for acceptance (sixty (60) days if no period is specified), executes the further contractual documents and gives the bond(s) required by the terms of the bid as accepted within the time specified (ten (10) days if no period is specified) after receipt of the forms by the principal; or (b) in the event of failure to execute such further contractual documents and give such bonds, pays the Government for any cost of procuring the work which exceeds the amount of the bid.

Each Surety executing this instrument agrees that its obligation is not impaired by any extension(s) of the time for acceptance of the bid that the Principal may grant to the Government. Notice to the surety(ies) of extension(s) are waived. However, waiver of the notice applies only to extensions aggregating not more than sixty (60) calendar days in addition to the period originally allowed for acceptance of the bid.

WITNESS:

The Principal and Surety(ies) executed this bid bond and affixed their seals on the above date.

PRINCIPAL

SIGNATURE(S)	1. (Seal)	2. (Seal)	3. (Seal)	Corporate Seal
NAME(S) & TITLE(S) *(Typed)*	1.	2.	3.	

INDIVIDUAL SURETY(IES)

SIGNATURE(S)	1. (Seal)	2. (Seal)
NAME(S) *(Typed)*	1.	2.

CORPORATE SURETY(IES)

SURETY A	NAME & ADDRESS		STATE OF INC.	LIABILITY LIMIT ($)	Corporate Seal
	SIGNATURE(S)	1.	2.		
	NAME(S) & TITLE(S) *(Typed)*	1.	2.		

AUTHORIZED FOR LOCAL REPRODUCTION
Previous edition is usable

STANDARD FORM 24 (REV. 10-98)
Prescribed by GSA - FAR (48 CFR) 53.228(a)

Figure 6.25 Bid bond *(continued on next page)*

			STATE OF INC.	LIABILITY LIMIT ($)	
SURETY B	NAME & ADDRESS				Corporate Seal
	SIGNATURE(S)	1.	2.		
	NAME(S) & TITLE(S) (Typed)	1.	2.		
			STATE OF INC.	LIABILITY LIMIT ($)	
SURETY C	NAME & ADDRESS				Corporate Seal
	SIGNATURE(S)	1.	2.		
	NAME(S) & TITLE(S) (Typed)	1.	2.		
			STATE OF INC.	LIABILITY LIMIT ($)	
SURETY D	NAME & ADDRESS				Corporate Seal
	SIGNATURE(S)	1.	2.		
	NAME(S) & TITLE(S) (Typed)	1.	2.		
			STATE OF INC.	LIABILITY LIMIT ($)	
SURETY E	NAME & ADDRESS				Corporate Seal
	SIGNATURE(S)	1.	2.		
	NAME(S) & TITLE(S) (Typed)	1.	2.		
			STATE OF INC.	LIABILITY LIMIT ($)	
SURETY F	NAME & ADDRESS				Corporate Seal
	SIGNATURE(S)	1.	2.		
	NAME(S) & TITLE(S) (Typed)	1.	2.		
			STATE OF INC.	LIABILITY LIMIT ($)	
SURETY G	NAME & ADDRESS				Corporate Seal
	SIGNATURE(S)	1.	2.		
	NAME(S) & TITLE(S) (Typed)	1.	2.		

INSTRUCTIONS

1. This form is authorized for use when a bid guaranty is required. Any deviation from this form will require the written approval of the Administrator of General Services.

2. Insert the full legal name and business address of the Principal in the space designated "Principal" on the face of the form. An authorized person shall sign the bond. Any person signing in a representative capacity (e.g., an attorney-in-fact) must furnish evidence of authority if that representative is not a member of the firm, partnership, or joint venture, or an officer of the corporation involved.

3. The bond may express penal sum as a percentage of the bid price. In these cases, the bond may state a maximum dollar limitation (e.g., (e.g., 20% of the bid price but the amount not to exceed_____ dollars).

4. (a) Corporations executing the bond as sureties must appear on the Department of the Treasury's list of approved sureties and must act within the limitation listed therein. where more than one corporate surety is involved, their names and addresses shall appear in the spaces (Surety A, Surety B, etc.) headed "CORPORATE SURETY(IES)." In the space designed "SURETY(IES)" on the face of the form, insert only the letter identification of the sureties.

   (b) Where individual sureties are involved, a completed Affidavit of Individual surety (Standard Form 28), for each individual surety, shall accompany the bond. The Government may require the surety to furnish additional substantiating information concerning its financial capability.

5. Corporations executing the bond shall affix their corporate seals. Individuals shall execute the bond opposite the word "Corporate Seal"; and shall affix an adhesive seal if executed in Maine, New Hampshire, or any other jurisdiction requiring adhesive seals.

6. Type the name and title of each person signing this bond in the space provided.

7. In its application to negotiated contracts, the terms "bid" and "bidder" shall include "proposal" and "offeror."

STANDARD FORM 24 (REV. 10-98) **BACK**

Figure 6.25 *(continued from previous page)* Bid bond

REVISED: MAY 2002
EFFECTIVE DATE: JULY 1, 2002

COUNTY OF PRINCE WILLIAM
DEPARTMENT OF PUBLIC WORKS

UNIT PRICE LIST
FOR
PERFORMANCE BONDS, LANDSCAPING ESCROWS, AND SILTATION & EROSION CONTROL ESCROWS

*PROJECT NAME:*_____

*P.W.C. FILE #:*_____   *DATE PREPARED:*_____

NOTE: This form is to be used to estimate performance bond, landscaping escrow and soil erosion escrow prices posted with Prince William County. These prices do not include items that are to be bonded separately with the Virginia Department of Transportation.

1. MOBILIZATION/DEMOBILIZATION OF CONSTRUCTION EQUIPMENT

Mobilization/Demobilization   @ Lump Sum $5, 000.00 (min.)

2. STORM DRAINAGE

A. STRUCTURES

QUANTITY		COST
_____ DI-1	@$2,000 EA	_____
_____ DI-3	@ 2,000 EA	_____
_____ DI-4	@ 4,000 EA	_____
_____ YI-1	@ 2,200 EA	_____
_____ MH-1	@ 1,800 EA	_____
_____ MH-2	@ 2,200 EA	_____
_____ JB-1	@ 4,000 EA	_____
_____ DI-7	@ 2,700 EA	_____

SUB-TOTAL $_____

Figure 6.26 Unit price list for services *(continued on next page)*

QUANTITY	COST	QUANTITY	COST
_____ 12"0 @$28 LF	_____	_____ 36"0 @ $ 75 LF	_____
_____ 15"0 @ 32 LF	_____	_____ 42"0 @ 90 LF	_____
_____ 18"0 @ 36 LF	_____	_____ 48"0 @ 105 LF	_____
_____ 21"0 @ 40 LF	_____	_____ 54"0 @ 125 LF	_____
_____ 24"0 @ 44 LF	_____	_____ 60"0 @ 155 LF	_____
_____ 27"0 @ 50 LF		_____ 66"0 @ 175 LF	_____
_____ 30"0 @ 56 LF		_____ 72"0 @ 210 LF	_____
_____ 33"0 @ 65 LF			

C. END WALLS

QUANTITY	COST	QUANTITY	COST
_____ 12"0 @ $500 EA	_____	_____ 36"0 @ $ 1,800 EA	_____
_____ 15"0 @ 600 EA	_____	_____ 42"0 @ 2,100 EA	_____
_____ 18"0 @ 700 EA	_____	_____ 48"0 @ 2,300 EA	_____
_____ 21"0 @ 850 EA	_____	_____ 54"0 @ 2,700 EA	_____
_____ 24"0 @ 1,100 EA	_____	_____ 60"0 @ 3,000 EA	_____
_____ 27"0 @ 1,300 EA	_____	_____ 66"0 @ 3,400 EA	_____
_____ 30"0 @ 1,450 EA	_____	_____ 72"0 @ 3,900 EA	_____
_____ 33"0 @ 1,600 EA	_____		

D. END SECTIONS (ES - 1)

QUANTITY	COST	QUANTITY	COST
_____ 12"0 @ $350 EA	_____	_____ 27"0 @ $ 650 EA	_____
_____ 15"0 @ 400 EA	_____	_____ 30"0 @ 750 EA	_____
_____ 18"0 @ 450 EA	_____	_____ 33"0 @ 850 EA	_____
_____ 21"0 @ 500 EA	_____	_____ 36"0 @ 1,000 EA	_____
_____ 24"0 @ 550 EA	_____		

E. CORRUGATED METAL PIPE

QUANTITY	COST	QUANTITY	COST
_____ 12"0 @ $ 20 LF	_____	_____ 36"0 @ $ 65 LF	_____
_____ 15"0 @ 25 LF	_____	_____ 42"0 @ 75 LF	_____
_____ 18"0 @ 35 LF	_____	_____ 48"0 @ 85 LF	_____
_____ 24"0 @ 45 LF	_____	_____ 54"0 @ 100 LF	_____
_____ 30"0 @ 55 LF	_____	_____ 60"0 @ 115 LF	_____

F. END SECTION (ES -2)

QUANTITY	COST	QUANTITY	COST
_____ 15"0 @ $300 EA	_____	_____ 36"0 @ $ 600 EA	_____
_____ 18"0 @ 350 EA	_____	_____ 42"0 @ $ 700 EA	_____
_____ 24"0 @ 400 EA	_____	_____ 48"0 @ $ 800 EA	_____
_____ 30"0 @ 450 EA	_____		

SUB-TOTAL $_____   SUB-TOTAL $_____

SUB-TOTAL FOR THIS PAGE $_____

Figure 6.26   *(continued from previous page)* Unit price list for services

G. AD N -12 (HDPE)*

QUANTITY			**COST**
_____12"0	@ $ 20 LF		_____
_____15"0	@ 25 LF		_____
_____18"0	@ 30 LF		_____
_____24"0	@ 40 LF		_____
_____30"0	@ 45 LF		_____
_____36"0	@ 50 LF		_____
_____42"0	@ 55 LF		_____
_____48"0	@ 70 LF		_____
_____60"0	@ 100 LF		_____

SUB-TOTAL $_____

H. STORMWATER MANAGEMENT/BMP FACILITIES (See note #5)

QUANTITY			**COST**
_____	Excavation	@ $ 8.00 CY	_____
_____	Embankment (Fill Material)**	@ 15.00 CY	_____

**STORM DRAINAGE PIPE
(RCP, CMP, PVC, Riser)**

_____		@ LF	_____
_____		@ LF	_____
_____		@ LF	_____

**STORM DRAINAGE STRUCTURES
(DI-7, MH-1, MH-2, etc.)**

_____		@ EA	_____
_____		@ EA	_____
_____	Concrete Cradle*	@ 22 LF	_____
_____	End Wall	@ EA	_____
_____	End Section	@ EA	_____
_____	Anti-seep collars	@ EA	_____
	($100 per 12"0 increments)		
_____	Trash Rack	@ EA	_____
	($300 per 12"0 increments)		

SUB-TOTAL $_____

SUB-TOTAL FOR THIS PAGE $_____

Figure 6.26   *(continued from previous page)* Unit price list for services

SPILLWAY LINING

<u>QUANTITY</u>   <u>COST</u>

_____   Seed, Fertilizer & Mulch   @ $0.50 SY(up to 1Ac)   _____
                       $200 Min.   @ 0.40 SY(1 to 5 Ac)   _____
                                                                     @ 0.30 SY (5 + Ac)   _____
_____   Sod   @ 6.00 SY   _____
_____   Hydraulic Cem. Conc. - 4" depth   @ 3.00 SF   _____
_____   Bituminous Concrete -1" depth   @ 2.50 SY   _____
_____   Rip-Rap   @ 5.50 SF   _____
_____   Grouted Rip-Rap   @ 7.00 SF   _____

_____   Erosion Control Stone (EC-1)   @$90.00 TON   _____
_____   #57 - Coarse Aggregate   @ 22.00 TON   _____
_____   Porous Pavement   @ 16.50 SY   _____
_____   4' High Chain Link Fence   @ 12.00 LF   _____
                       (#9 gauge or better, including braces, end posts and gate)
_____   6' High Chain Link Fence   @ 18.00 LF   _____
                       (#9 gauge or better, including braces, end posts and gate)
_____   SWM Sign (WATER RISES RAPIDLY)   @ 200 EA   _____

                                                                        SUB-TOTAL $_____

I. MISCELLANEOUS DRAINAGE ITEMS

_____   Box Culvert   @ $ 600 CY of conc.   _____
_____   Energy Dissipater   @ 1,500 EA   _____
_____   Wing Walls*   @   600 CY of conc.   _____

DITCHES

_____   Roadside standard ditches   @ $ 6.00 LF   _____
                       (Seed, fertilize and mulch)
_____   Sod Ditches   @   7.50 LF   _____
_____   Paved Ditches   @   6.00 SF   _____
_____   Filter Cloth Fabric & Gabion Stone @   4.00 SF   _____
_____   Rip-rap   @   6.50 SF   _____
_____   Grouted Rip-rap   @   8.00 SF   _____
_____   Paved Flume   @   11.00 SF   _____
_____   Flush the Drainage System   @   180/Hr   _____
                                                                     (Minimum 4 Hrs)

                                                                        SUB-TOTAL $_____

                                                        SUB-TOTAL FOR THIS PAGE $_____

Figure 6.26 *(continued from previous page)* Unit price list for services

3. CONSTRUCTION WITHIN THE RIGHT-OF-WAY AND/OR EASEMENTS

A. SITE WORK

QUANTITY		COST
_____ Clear & Grub	@ $8,500 AC	_____
_____ Excavation	@ 8.00 CY	_____
_____ Embankment**	@ 15.00 CY	_____
_____ Rock Excavation	@ 30.00 CY	_____
_____ Slope Stabilization - Hydroseeding (3:1 or flatter) $1,000 Min.	@ $0.50 SY (up to 1 Ac)	_____
	@ 0.40 SY (1+ to 5 Ac)	_____
	@ 0.30 SY (5+ Acres)	_____
_____ Slope Stab. - Jute Mesh, Matting, Blankets, etc. (Between 2:1 to 3:1) $200 Min.	@ 5.00 SY	_____
_____ Slope Stab. - Sod (Between 2:1 to 3:1) $200 Min	@ 6.00 SY	_____
_____ Steep Slopes (Grading and Stabilization with Jute Mesh, Netting, Blankets, etc.)	@ 10.00 SY	_____
	SUB-TOTAL $_____	

B. SUBGRADE, SUBBASE AND BASE COURSE ITEMS

QUANTITY (For streets dedicated for public use)   COST
Identify quantities separately for each street (Use Page 5a)

_____ Subgrade preparation*	@ $ 1.50 SY	_____
Subbase & Base Course		
_____ Aggregate (21A/21B)	@ 1.00 SY Per Inch Depth	_____
_____ Bituminous Concrete	@ 2.50 SY Per Inch Depth	_____
Class A Prime & Double Seal		
_____ Surface Treatment	@ 4.00 SY	_____
_____ Gravel Shoulders	@ 4.50 SY (4" Depth)	_____
Underdrains:		
_____ UD-1	@ 14.00 LF	_____
_____ UD-2	@ 16.00 LF	_____
_____ UD-3	@ 15.00 LF	_____
_____ UD-4	@ 12.00 LF	_____
_____ Soil Cem. Stabilization (4%)	@ 8.00 SY (6" Depth)	_____
_____ Lime Stabilization (10%)	@ 7.00 SY (6" Depth)	_____
_____ Cement Treated Aggregate	@ 1.50 SY Per Inch Depth	_____
	SUB-TOTAL $_____	
	SUB-TOTAL FOR THIS PAGE $_____	

Figure 6.26   *(continued from previous page)* Unit price list for services

C. SUBBASE AND BASE COURSE ITEMS

(For private streets, travel lanes, and parking areas)

<u>QUANTITY</u>   <u>COST</u>

Subbase & Base Course
_____ Aggregate (21A)   @ $ 1.00 SY Per Inch Depth   _____
_____ Bituminous Concrete   @   2.50 SY Per Inch Depth   _____
Class A Prime & Double Seal
_____ Surface Treatment   @   4.00 SY Per Inch Depth   _____
_____ Gravel Shoulders   @   4.50 SY (4" Depth)   _____
_____ Cement Stabilization (4%)   @ <u>10.00</u> SY (6" Depth)   _____
_____ Lime Stabilization (10%)   @   <u>9.00</u> SY (6" Depth)   _____

SUB-TOTAL $_____

D. ENTRANCES AND PIPE STEMS

_____ DE-1   @ $1,000 EA
_____ DE-2   @   800 EA   _____
_____ DE-3*   @   800 EA   _____
_____ DE-4*   @   800 EA   _____
_____ PP-1 (1 lot)   @   <u>800</u> EA   _____
_____ PP-1 (2 - 5 lots)   @   1,100 EA   _____
_____ PP-2 (1 lot)   @   600 EA   _____
_____ PP-2 (2 - 5 lots)   @   800 EA   _____
_____ CG-9D or equal   @   3,500 EA   _____
30' Width   _____
_____ CG-9D or equal   @   5,000 EA
40' Width   _____
_____ CG-10A or equal   @   2,500 EA
30' Width   _____
_____ CG-10A or equal   @   3,500 EA
40' Width   _____
_____ CG-11   @   1,500 EA
Concrete Entrance   _____
_____ Valley Gutter   @   40 SY   _____
_____ Pipestem Driveway - 10' (1 lot)   @   <u>40</u> LF   _____
_____ Pipestem Driveway - 18' (2-5 lots) @   <u>55</u> LF   _____

SUB-TOTAL   _____

SUB-TOTAL FOR THIS PAGE   _____

Figure 6.26 *(continued from previous page)* Unit price list for services

E. MISCELLANEOUS CONSTRUCTION ITEMS

QUANTITY   **COST**

_____	Sidewalk (4' Width)	@ $	12 LF	_____
_____	Header Curb (CG-2/CG-3)	@	15 LF	_____
_____	Curb & Gutter	@	20 LF	_____
_____	CG-12 (Exposed Aggregate)	@	55 SY	_____
_____	Bicycle Trail/Walkway	@	4 SF	_____
_____	Raised Concrete Median (MS-1A)	@	50 SY	_____
_____	Trail (Wood Chip)*	@	17 SY	_____
_____	Trail (Stone Dust)*	@	12 SY	_____

Retaining Walls

_____	Timber	@	20 SF	_____
_____	Crib	@	25 SF	_____
_____	Reinforced Earth	@	30 SF	_____
_____	Reinforced Concrete	@	45 SF	_____
_____	Excavation for tiebacks in walls in cut areas	@	8 CY	_____
_____	Anti-graffiti Paint* (concrete retaining walls only)	@	10 SF (Min. $2,000)	_____

_____	Guardrail	@	20 LF	_____
_____	GR-7 NCHRP 350	@	2,000 EA	_____
_____	GR-9	@	3,000 EA	_____

_____	Address Sign (Entrance to Pipestems)	@	175 EA	_____
_____	Street Name Sign	@	225 EA	_____
_____	Traffic Control Sign	@	175 EA	_____
_____	HC Parking Space Sign*	@	175 EA	_____
_____	Roadside Delineators (ED-1)	@	50 EA	_____
_____	Hand Rail (HR-1)	@	55 LF	_____
_____	Pavement Marking (Paint)	@	1 SF	_____
_____	Pavement Marking (Thermoplastic)	@	2.50 SF	_____
_____	Traffic Barricade (TB-1)	@	500 EA	_____
_____	Street Lighting	@	3,000 EA	_____
_____	Utilities Relocation*		(Min. $40,000) (or provide an estimate from utility company)	_____
_____	P.E. Certified "As-Built" Plans		Lump Sum (Min. $5,000)	_____

SUB-TOTAL _____

SUB-TOTAL FOR THIS PAGE _____

Figure 6.26 *(continued from previous page)* Unit price list for services

4. SANITARY SEWER & WATER LINE CONSTRUCTION

QUANTITY   **COST**

_____	Fire Hydrant	@ $ 2,500 EA	
_____	Sanitary Sewer Manhole	@ 4,700 EA	_____

WATER MAIN (Exclusive of Fire Hydrants)

_____	4"0 DIP	@$ 38 LF	
_____	6"0 DIP	@ 50 LF	_____
_____	8"0 DIP	@ 62 LF	_____
_____	12"0 DIP	@ 74 LF	_____
_____	16"0 DIP	@ 90 LF	_____
_____	18"0 DIP	@ 100 LF	_____
_____	Fire Hydrant Assembly	@ 2,500 EA	_____
_____	Meter Crock	@ 1,030 EA	_____

SANITARY SEWER PIPE LINE (Exclusive of Manhole Structures)

_____	8"0 PVC	@ $ 60 LF	
_____	8"0 DIP	@ 70 LF	_____
_____	10"0 PVC	@ 75 LF	_____
_____	10"0 DIP	@ 85 LF	_____
_____	12"0 PVC	@ 135 LF	_____
_____	12"0 DIP	@ 145 LF	_____
_____	15"0 DIP	@ 175 LF	_____

For sizes larger than 15"0, add $4.00 per inch increase in diameter.

SUB-TOTAL $_____

TOTAL CONSTRUCTION COST $_____

(Pages 1 thru 8)

5. MISCELLANEOUS COSTS

A. Administrative Cost - 15% of the total construction cost, not to exceed $50,000 $_____

B. Inflation Cost - Compounded annually at 3.0% per year of the total Construction Cost   _____

Total Performance Bond Amount $_____

Figure 6.26 *(continued from previous page)* Unit price list for services

6. <u>LANDSCAPING ESCROW</u>

A. DECIDUOUS TREES

<u>QUANTITY</u>   <u>COST</u>

_____	4' - 5'	@ $ 75 EA	_____
_____	5' - 6'	@ 150 EA	_____
_____	1" - 1½ " or 1½ - 2"	@ 150 EA	_____
_____	2" - 2½ " or 2½ - 3"	@ 230 EA	_____
_____	3" - 3½ " or 3½ - 4"	@ 350 EA	_____

B. EVERGREEN TREES

_____	4' - 5'	@ $ 80 EA	_____
_____	5' - 6'	@ 100 EA	_____
_____	6' - 7'	@ 150 EA	_____
_____	7' - 8'	@ 200 EA	_____
_____	8' - 10'	@ 250 EA	_____

C. SHRUBS

_____	18" - 24"	@ $ 35 EA	_____
_____	24" - 30"	@ 50 EA	_____

TOTAL COST $_____

Figure 6.26 *(continued from previous page)* Unit price list for services

7. SILTATION AND EROSION CONTROL ESCROWS

_____	Diversion Dike	@ $ 5 LF	_____
_____	Straw Bale Barrier	@ 5 LF	_____
_____	Cleaning out SWM Facilities, Silt Traps, and Silt Basins	@ 500/Hr. Lump Sum (Min. $20,000)	_____
_____	Silt Fence	@ 5 LF	_____
_____	Super Silt Fence	@ 15 LF	_____
_____	Sod	@ 6 SY	_____
_____	Seed, Fertilizer & Mulch ($200 Min.)	@ .50 SY (Up to 1 Ac)	_____
		.40 SY (1+ to 5 Ac)	_____
		.30 SY (5+ Acres)	_____
_____	Steep Slopes (Grading and Stabilization with jute mesh, netting, blankets, etc.)	@ 10 SY	_____
_____	Coarse Aggregates (#1 or #57)	@ 22 TON	_____
_____	Inlet Protection	@ 120 EA	_____
_____	Check Dam	@ 125 EA	_____
_____	Temp. Construction Entrance	@ 1,000 EA	_____
_____	Wash Rack	@ 2,000 EA	_____
_____	Temp. Sediment Trap	@ 500 EA (Drain. area up to 1 Ac)	_____
		@ 1,000 EA (Drainage area 1-2 Ac)	_____
		@ 1,800 EA (Drainage area 2-3 Ac)	_____
_____	Temporary Sediment Basin:	By itemized cost	_____
_____	Channel Diversion	By itemized cost	_____
_____	6' Chain-link Safety Fence	@ 18 LF	_____
_____	4' Plastic Orange Safety Fence	@ 2 LF	_____
_____	Yard utility refurbishment	@ 500 EA Single Family Lot	_____
_____		@ $	_____
_____		@	_____
_____		@	_____

TOTAL COST $ _____

ADMINISTRATIVE COST (15% of Total Cost) _____

TOTAL SILTATION & EROSION CONTROL ESCROW AMOUNT _____

I hereby certify that the above is my best estimate of the quantities and current cost of bondable improvements, landscaping items, and Siltation & Erosion Control Escrow in this subdivision or site plan.

_____   _____
PREPARER'S SIGNATURE   TELEPHONE #

_____   _____
NAME (print)   COMPANY OR FIRM

Figure 6.26 *(continued from previous page)* Unit price list for services

NOTES:

1. All changes to the Unit Price List are highlighted. The revised prices are underlined. Items identified with * indicate the new items added to Prince William County's previous "Unit Price List" of May 1999.

2. For items identified with ** the quantity for the embankment material is the net difference of total fill material needed and cut material available at the project site, if excavated or cut material is suitable for embankment.

3. The excavation and embankment costs include the necessary grading, spreading and/or compaction of soil in accordance with County and State Standards and Specifications.

4. For some of the items on page 3 of this form, the unit prices are not provided. Please refer to the appropriate section of this form to determine the applicable unit prices for those items, if necessary.

5. The unit cost for each of the items in this Unit Price List is the installation cost which includes factors such as excavation, bedding, backfilling, compaction, form work, etc.

6. Inflation has been calculated based on Northern Virginia Consumer Price Index of the Washington, D.C., area provided by the Bureau of Labor and Statistics.

7. Whoever certifies the site development plans must also certify the total cost of the bonded items, landscaping escrow and siltation and erosion control escrow and must sign on "Preparer's Signature" on page 10 of this form.

Figure 6.26 *(continued from previous page)* Unit price list for services

REPLACEMENT / REPAIR ITEMS
(To be used only for performance bond reduction / extension requests)

<u>QUANTITY</u>				<u>COST</u>
_____	Relocate utility poles	@ $	6,500 (min.)	_____
_____	Remove basketball pole(s) from the right-of-way	@	200 EA	_____
_____	Remove fence from the right-of-way from the right-of-way	@	5 LF	_____
_____	Remove trees, shrubs, landscaping from the right-of-way	@	Lump Sum	_____
_____	Cut out and patch pavement and base	@	15 SY	_____
_____	Replace curb and gutter	@	25 LF	_____
_____	Replace sidewalk - 4' width	@	20 LF	_____
_____	Re-establish ditch line	@	5 LF (min. $200)	_____
_____	Place additional stone on shoulders	@	1 SY/in. depth	_____
_____	Relocate / reset mailboxes	@	150 EA	_____
_____	Straighten out bent ends of driveway entrance pipes	@	100 EA Pipe	_____
_____	Remove and replace entrance pipe	@	35 LF	_____
_____	Lower / raise entrance pipe within the right-of-way	@	300 EA	_____
_____	Clean out driveway entrance pipes	@	100 EA Pipe (min. $200)	_____
_____	Readjust manhole tops	@	300 EA	_____
_____	Remove form material	@	100 (min)	_____
_____	Install missing steps in storm storm drainage structures	@	100 EA	_____
_____	Parge storm drainage structures	@	200 EA	_____
_____	Paint metal parts	@	50 EA	_____
_____	Place additional rip-rap	@	50 SY	_____
_____	Place additional grouted rip-rap	@	63 SY	_____
_____	Place additional guard rail not shown on the plans	@	18 LF	_____
_____	Place additional paved ditch not shown on the plans	@	6 SF	_____
_____	Place additional signs within the the right-of-way	@	100 EA	_____
_____	Mow grass within the right-of-way and storm drainage easements	@	Lump Sum	_____
_____	Remove construction debris from the project site	@	Lump Sum	_____
_____	other items	@		_____
_____	other items	@		_____

SUB-TOTAL $_____

Figure 6.26   *(continued from previous page)* Unit price list for services

Form RD 1942-19   UNITED STATES DEPARTMENT OF AGRICULTURE   FORM APPROVED
(Rev. 10-96)   RURAL DEVELOPMENT   OMB NO. 0575-0015

AGREEMENT FOR ENGINEERING SERVICES

This Agreement, made this _____ day of _____ , 19 _____ ,

by and between _____ , hereafter referred to as the OWNER,

and _____ , hereinafter referred to as the ENGINEER:

THE OWNER intends to construct a _____

_____in_____County, State of_____
which may be paid for in part with financial assistance from the United States of America acting through Rural Development of the United States Department of Agriculture, pursuant to the consolidated Farm and Rural Development Act, (7 U.S.C. 1921 et seq.) and for which the ENGINEER agrees to perform the various professional engineering services for the design and construction of said system.

WITNESSETH:

That for and in consideration of the mutual covenants and promises between the parties hereto, it is hereby agreed:

SECTION A - ENGINEERING SERVICES

The ENGINEER shall furnish engineering services as follows:

1. The ENGINEER will conduct preliminary investigations, prepare preliminary drawings, provide a preliminary itemized list of probable construction costs effective as of the date of the preliminary report, and submit a preliminary engineering report following Rural Development instructions and guides.

2. The ENGINEER will furnish 10 copies of the preliminary engineering report, and layout maps to the OWNER.

3. The ENGINEER will attend conferences with the OWNER, representatives of Rural Development, or other interested parties as may be reasonably necessary.

4. After the preliminary engineering report has been reviewed and approved by the OWNER and by Rural Development and the OWNER directs the ENGINEER to proceed, the ENGINEER will perform the necessary design surveys, accomplish the detailed design of the project, prepare construction drawings, specifications and contract documents, and prepare a final cost estimate based on the final design for the entire system. It is also understood that if subsurface explorations (such as borings, soil tests, rock soundings and the like) are required, the ENGINEER will furnish coordination of said explorations without additional charge, but the costs incident to such explorations shall be paid for by the OWNER as set out in Section D hereof.

5. The contract documents furnished by the ENGINEER under Section A-4 shall utilize Rural Development-endorsed construction contract documents, including Rural Development General Conditions, Contract Change Orders, and partial payment estimates. All of these documents shall be subject to Rural Development approval. Copies of guide contract documents may be obtained from Rural Development.

6. Prior to the advertisement for bids, the ENGINEER will provide for each construction contract, not to exceed 10 copies of detailed drawings, specifications, and contract documents for use by the OWNER, appropriate Federal, State, and local agencies from whom approval of the project must be obtained. The cost of such drawings, specifications, and contract documents shall be included in the basic compensation paid to the ENGINEER.

7. The ENGINEER will furnish additional copies of the drawings, specifications and contract documents as required by prospective bidders, material suppliers, and other interested parties, but may charge them for the reasonable cost of such copies. Upon award of each contract, the ENGINEER will furnish to the OWNER five sets of the drawings, specifications and contract documents for execution. The cost of these sets shall be included in the basic compensation paid to the ENGINEER. Original documents, survey notes, tracings, and the like, except those furnished to the ENGINEER by the OWNER, are and shall remain the property of the ENGINEER.

Position 6   RD 1942-19 (Rev. 10-96)

Figure 6.27 Agreement for engineering services *(continued on next page)*

(Section A - continued)

8. The drawings prepared by the ENGINEER under the provisions of Section A-4 above shall be in sufficient detail to permit the actual location of the proposed improvements on the ground. The ENGINEER shall prepare and furnish to the OWNER without any additional compensation, three copies of a map(s) showing the general location of needed construction easements and permanent easements and the land to be acquired. Property surveys, property plats, property descriptions, abstracting and negotiations for land rights shall be accomplished by the OWNER, unless the OWNER requests, and the ENGINEER agrees to provide those services. In the event the ENGINEER is requested to provide such services, the ENGINEER shall be additionally compensated as set out in Section D hereof.

9. The ENGINEER will attend the bid opening and tabulate the bid proposals, make an analysis of the bids, and make recommendations for awarding contracts for construction.

10. The ENGINEER will review and approve, for conformance with the design concept, any necessary shop and working drawings furnished by contractors.

11. The ENGINEER will interpret the intent of the drawings and specifications to protect the OWNER against defects and deficiencies in construction on the part of the contractors. The ENGINEER will not, however, guarantee the performance by any contractor.

12. The ENGINEER will establish baselines for locating the work together with a suitable number of bench marks adjacent to the work as shown in the contract documents.

13. The ENGINEER will provide general engineering review of the work of the contractors as construction progresses to ascertain that the contractor is conforming with the design concept.

14. Unless notified by the OWNER in writing that the OWNER will provide for resident inspection, the ENGINEER will provide resident construction inspection. The ENGINEER'S undertaking hereunder shall not relieve the contractor of contractor's obligation to perform the work in conformity with the drawings and specifications and in a workmanlike manner; shall not make the ENGINEER an insurer of the contractor's performance; and shall not impose upon the ENGINEER any obligation to see that the work is performed in a safe manner.

15. The ENGINEER will cooperate and work closely with Rural Development representatives.

16. The ENGINEER will review the contractor's applications for progress and final payment and, when approved, submit same to the OWNER for payment.

17. The ENGINEER will prepare necessary contract change orders for approval of the OWNER, Rural Development, and others on a timely basis.

18. The ENGINEER will make a final review prior to the issuance of the statement of substantial completion of all construction and submit a written report to the OWNER and Rural Development. Prior to submitting the final pay estimate, the ENGINEER shall submit a statement of completion to and obtain the written acceptance of the facility from the OWNER and Rural Development.

19. The ENGINEER will provide the OWNER with one set of reproducible record (as-built) drawings, and two sets of prints at no additional cost to the OWNER. Such drawings will be based upon construction records provided by the contractor during construction and reviewed by the resident inspector and from the resident inspector's construction data.

20. If State statutes require notices and advertisements of final payment, the ENGINEER shall assist in their preparation.

21. The ENGINEER will be available to furnish engineering services and consultations necessary to correct unforeseen project operation difficulties for a period of one year after the date of statement of substantial completion of the facility. This service will include instruction of the OWNER in initial project operation and maintenance but will not include supervision of normal operation of the system. Such consultation and advice shall be furnished without additional charge except for travel and subsistence costs. The ENGINEER will assist the OWNER in performing a review of the project during the 11th month after the date of the certificate of substantial completion.

22. The ENGINEER further agrees to obtain and maintain, at the ENGINEER'S expense, such insurance as will protect the ENGINEER from claims under the Workman's Compensation Act and such comprehensive general liability insurance as will protect the OWNER and the ENGINEER from all claims for bodily injury, death, or property damage which may arise from the performance by the ENGINEER or by the ENGINEER'S employees of the ENGINEER'S functions and services required under this Agreement.

Figure 6.27 *(continued from previous page)* Agreement for engineering services

(Section A - continued)

23. The services called for in the Section A-1 and A-2 of this Agreement shall be completed and the report submitted within _____ calendar days from the date of authorization to proceed. After acceptance by the OWNER and Rural Development of the Preliminary Engineering Report and upon written authorization from the OWNER, the ENGINEER will complete final plans, specifications and contract documents and submit for approval of the OWNER, Rural Development and all State regulatory

agencies within _____ calendar days from the date of authorization unless otherwise agreed to by both parties.

If the above is not accomplished within the time period specified, this Agreement may be terminated by the OWNER. The time for completion will be extended by the OWNER for a reasonable time if completion is delayed due to unforeseeable causes beyond the control and without the fault or negligence of the ENGINEER.

SECTION B - COMPENSATION FOR ENGINEERING SERVICES

1. The OWNER shall compensate the ENGINEER for preliminary engineering services in the sum of

_____ Dollars ($ _____) after the review and approval of the preliminary engineering report by the OWNER and Rural Development.

2. The OWNER shall compensate the ENGINEER for design and contract administration engineering services in the amount of: (Select (a) or (b))

   (a) _____ Dollars ($ _____) or

   (b) As shown in Attachment 1

      When Attachment 1 is used to establish compensation for the design and contract administration services, the actual construction costs on which compensation is determined shall exclude legal fees, administrative costs, engineering fees, land rights, acquisition costs, water costs, and interest expense incurred during the construction period.

3. The compensation for preliminary engineering services, design and contract administration services shall be payable as follows:

   (a) A sum which equals seventy percent (70%) of the total compensation payable under Section B-1 and 2, after completion and submission of the construction drawings, specifications, cost estimates, and contract documents, and the acceptance of the same by OWNER and Rural Development.

   (b) A sum which, together with the compensation provided in Section B-3-(a) above, equals eighty percent (80%) of the compensation payable immediately after the construction contracts are awarded.

   (c) A sum equal to fifteen percent (15%) of the compensation will be paid on a monthly basis for general engineering review of the contractor's work during the construction period on percentage ratios identical to those approved by the ENGINEER as a basis upon which to make partial payments to the contractor(s). However, payment under this paragraph and of such additional sums as are due the ENGINEER by reason of any necessary adjustments in the payment computations will be in an amount so that the aggregate of all sums paid to the ENGINEER will equal ninety-five (95%) of the compensation. A final payment to equal 100 percent shall be made when it is determined that all services required by this Agreement have been completed except for the services set forth in Section A-21 hereof.

SECTION C - COMPENSATION FOR RESIDENT INSPECTION
AS SET FORTH IN SECTION A-14

When the ENGINEER provides resident inspection, the ENGINEER will, prior to the preconstruction conference, submit a resume of the resident inspector's qualifications, anticipated duties and responsibilities for approval by the OWNER and Rural Development. The OWNER agrees to pay the ENGINEER for such services in accordance with the schedule set out in Attachment 1. The ENGINEER will render to OWNER for such services an itemized bill, once each month, for compensation for such services performed hereunder during such period, the same to be due and payable by the OWNER to the ENGINEER on or before the 10th day of the following period.

Under normal construction circumstances, and for the proposed construction period of _____ days, the cost of

resident inspection is estimated to be $ _____ .

Figure 6.27 *(continued from previous page)* Agreement for engineering services

SECTION D - ADDITIONAL ENGINEERING SERVICES

In addition to the foregoing being performed, the following services may be provided UPON PRIOR WRITTEN AUTHORIZATION OF THE OWNER and written approval of Rural Development.

1. Site surveys for water treatment plants, sewage treatment works, dams, reservoirs, and other similar special surveys as may be required.

2. Laboratory tests, well tests, borings, specialized geological, soils, hydraulic, or other studies recommended by the ENGINEER.

3. Property surveys, detailed description of sites, maps, drawings, or estimates related thereto; assistance in negotiating for land and easement rights.

4. Necessary data and filing maps for water rights, water adjudication, and litigation.

5. Redesigns ordered by the OWNER after final plans have been accepted by the OWNER and Rural Development, except redesigns to reduce the project cost to within the funds available.

6. Appearances before courts or boards on matters of litigation or hearings related to the project.

7. Preparation of environment impact assessments or environmental impact statements.

8. Performance of detailed staking necessary for construction of the project in excess of the control staking set forth in Section A-12.

9. The ENGINEER further agrees to provide the operation and maintenance manual for facilities when required for

$ _____ .

Payment for the services specified in this Section D shall be as agreed in writing between the OWNER and approved by Rural Development prior to commencement of the work. Barring unforeseen circumstances, such payment is estimated not to exceed

$ _____ . The ENGINEER will render to OWNER for such services an itemized bill, separate from any other billing, once each month, for compensation for services performed hereunder during such period, the same to be due and payable by OWNER to the ENGINEER on or before the 10th day of the following period.

SECTION E - INTEREST ON UNPAID SUMS

If OWNER fails to make any payment due ENGINEER within 60 days for services and expenses and funds are available for the

project then the ENGINEER shall be entitled to interest at the rate of _____ percent per annum from said 60th day, not to exceed an annual rate of 12 percent.

SECTION F - SPECIAL PROVISIONS

Figure 6.27 *(continued from previous page)* Agreement for engineering services

SECTION G - APPROVAL BY RURAL DEVELOPMENT

This Agreement shall not become effective until approved by Rural Development. Such approval shall be evidenced by the signature of a duly authorized representative of Rural Development in the space provided at the end of this Agreement. The approval so evidenced by Rural Development shall in no way commit Rural Development to render financial assistance to the OWNER and is without liability for any payment hereunder, but in the event such assistance is provided, approval shall signify that the provisions of this Agreement are consistent with the requirements of Rural Development.

IN WITNESS WHEREOF, the parties hereto have executed, or caused to be executed by their duly authorized officials, this Agreement in duplicate on the respective dates indicated below.

(SEAL)   OWNER:

                                                            By _____

ATTEST _____   Type Name _____

                                                            Title _____

Type Name _____   Date _____

Title _____

(SEAL)

                                                            ENGINEER:

ATTEST _____   By _____

                                                            Type Name _____

Type Name _____   Title _____

Title _____   Date _____

APPROVED:

RURAL DEVELOPMENT

By _____

Type Name _____

Title _____

Date _____

Figure 6.27   *(continued from previous page)* Agreement for engineering services

INTERIM AGREEMENT

(For use only when OWNER is not legally organized on the date the Agreement for Engineering Services is executed.)

In lieu of the execution of the foregoing Agreement for Engineering Services dated the _____ day of

_____ , 19 ___ , by the party designated as OWNER therein, the undersigned, hereinafter referred to as INTERIM PARTIES, have executed this Interim Agreement in consideration of the services described in Section A-1 through A-3, inclusive, of said Agreement for Engineering Services to be performed by the ENGINEER, and the ENGINEER agrees to accept this Interim Agreement as evidenced by ENGINEER'S execution hereof contemporaneously with the execution of the Agreement for Engineering Services. The ENGINEER also agrees to perform the services set forth in Section A-1 through A-3, inclusive, of said Agreement in consideration of the sum stated in Section B-1 of said Agreement be paid in the manner set forth therein.

It is anticipated that the OWNER shall promptly become a legal entity with full authority to accept and execute said Agreement for Engineering Services and that the OWNER, after becoming so qualified, shall promptly take such action necessary to adopt, ratify, execute, and become bound by the Agreement for Engineering Services. The ENGINEER agrees that upon such due execution of the Agreement for Engineering Services by the OWNER, the INTERIM PARTIES automatically will be relieved of any responsibility or of liability assumed by their execution of this Interim Agreement, and that the ENGINEER will hold the OWNER solely responsible for performance of the terms and conditions imposed upon the OWNER by the Agreement for Engineering Services, including the payment of all sums specified in Section B-1 of said Agreement.

If the OWNER is not legally organized, or if after being duly organized it fails or refuses to adopt, ratify, and execute the Agreement for Engineering Services within 30 days from the date it becomes legally organized and qualified to do so, or if for any other reason the project fails to proceed beyond the preliminary stage described in Section A-1 through A-3 inclusive, of said Agreement, the INTERIM PARTIES agree to pay ENGINEER for such preliminary engineering services, an amount not to exceed the sum specified therefor in Section B-1 of said Agreement.

IN WITNESS WHEREOF, the parties hereto have executed, or caused to be executed by their duly authorized officials, this Agreement

in duplicate this _____ day of _____ , 19 ___ .

_____   _____
                    OWNER   ENGINEER

Figure 6.27 *(continued from previous page)* Agreement for engineering services

Chapter 7

Managing Your Development

Managing your development can be a daunting task. It does not have to be. If you have good organizational skills, the process can go very well. The process of managing a project can run very smoothly. However, this is usually not the case. Why? Because most developers are sloppy with their paperwork.

How important is the paperwork? It is very important. How valuable is the paperwork? It's not worth any more than the character of the individuals signing on the dotted line. In truth, most contracts are merely a false sense of security. Many professionals consider the contract process to be a method without means. This, of course, is not always true.

You are always better off if you have clear contracts and management documents. Will they result in success for you? Not necessarily, but they do help. Commitment between the parties of an agreement is what counts, but the paper trail can mean a lot if you go to court. Leaving out the legal issues, having a documented trail of papers in the appropriate files will make your business easier to manage. This chapter will show you some samples of the types of paperwork that can make your life easier and more profitable.

Your Company Name
Your Company Address
Your Company Phone and Fax Numbers

ADDENDUM

This addendum is an integral part of the contract dated _____,

between the Contractor, _____,

and the Customer(s), _____,

for the work being done on real estate commonly known as _____.

The undersigned parties hereby agree to the following: _____

_____

_____

_____

_____

_____

_____

_____

_____

_____

The above constitutes the only additions to the above-mentioned contract, no verbal agreements or other changes shall be valid unless made in writing and signed by all parties.

_____   _____
Contractor   Date   Customer
Date

                                          _____
                                          Customer   Date

Figure 7.1 Typical addendum to a contract

Your Company Name
Your Company Address
Your Company Phone and Fax Numbers

CANCEL ORDER

Date: _____

To: _____

_____

_____

I refer to our purchase order or contract dated _____, 19 _____, as attached.

Under said order, the goods were to be shipped by _____, 19 _____.

Because you failed to ship the goods within the required time, we cancel the order and reserve such further rights and remedies as we may have, including damage claims under the Uniform Commercial Code.

If said goods are in transit, they shall be refused and returned at your expense under your shipping instructions.

Sincerely,

_____

Title: _____

Figure 7.2 Cancellation of backordered goods

Your Company Name
Your Company Address
Your Company Phone and Fax Numbers

LETTER SOLICITING BIDS FROM SUBCONTRACTORS

Date: _____

Subcontractor address: _____

_____

_____

Dear: _____

I am soliciting bids for the work listed below, and I would like to offer you the opportunity to participate in the bidding. If you are interested in giving quoted prices for the <u>labor / material</u> for this job, please let me hear from you. The job will start _____. Financing has been arranged and the job will be started on schedule. Your quote, if you choose to enter one, must be received no later than _____.

The proposed work is as follows: _____

_____

_____

_____

Thank you for your time and consideration in this request.

Sincerely,

Your Name
Title

Figure 7.3 Letter soliciting bids from subcontractors

Your Company Name
Your Company Address
Your Company Phone and Fax Numbers

BID REQUEST

Contractor's name: _____

Contractor's address: _____

Contractor's city/state/zip: _____

Contractor's phone number: _____

Job location: _____

Plans and specifications dated: _____

Bid requested from: _____

Type of work: _____

Description of material to be quoted: _____

_____

_____

All quotes to be based on attached plans and specifications. No substitutions allowed without

written consent of customer.

Please provide quoted prices for the following: _____

_____

_____

_____

_____

All bids must be submitted by: _____

Figure 7.4 Bid request form

Your Company Name
Your Company Address
Your Company Phone and Fax Numbers

NOTICE OF BREACH OF CONTRACT

Date: _____

To: _____   From: _____

_____   _____

_____   _____

TAKE NOTICE that under Contract made _____, 19 _____, as evidenced by the following documents: _____, we are hereby holding you IN BREACH for the following reasons: _____

_____

_____

If your Breach is not cured within _____ days (i.e., cure must be completed by _____, 19 _____), we will take all further actions necessary to mitigate our damages and protect our rights, which may include, but are not necessarily limited to, the right to Cover" by obtaining substitute performance and chargeback to you of all additional costs and damages incurred.

This Notice is made under the Uniform Commercial Code (if applicable) and all other applicable laws. All rights are hereby reserved, none of which are waived. Any forbearance or temporary waiver from enforcement shall not constitute permanent waiver or waiver of any other right.

You are urged to cure your Breach forthwith.

_____
Developer

By: _____
        Authorized Signatory

Figure 7.5   Notice of breach of contract

Your Company Name
Your Company Address
Your Company Phone and Fax Numbers

CANCEL ORDER

Date: _____

To: _____

_____

_____

I refer to our purchase order or contract dated _____, 19 _____, as attached.

Under said order, the goods were to be shipped by _____, 19 _____.

Because you failed to ship the goods within the required time, we cancel the order and reserve such further rights and remedies as we may have, including damage claims under the Uniform Commercial Code.

If said goods are in transit, they shall be refused and returned at your expense under your shipping instructions.

Sincerely,

_____

Title: _____

Figure 7.6   Cancel order

Your Company Name
Your Company Address
Your Company Phone and Fax Numbers

CODE VIOLATION NOTIFICATION

Contractor: _____

Contractor's address: _____

Contractor's city/state/zip: _____

Contractor's phone number: _____

Job location: _____

Date: _____

Type of work: _____

Subcontractor: _____

Address: _____

OFFICIAL NOTIFICATION OF CODE VIOLATIONS

On _____, 19 _____, I was notified by the local code enforcement officer of code violations in the work performed by your company. The violations must be corrected within _____ (___) business days, as per our contract dated _____, 19 _____. Please contact the codes officer for a detailed explanation of the violations and required corrections. If the violations are not corrected within the allotted time, you may be penalized, as per our contract, for your actions in delaying the completion of this project. Thank you for your prompt attention to this matter.

_____   _____
Developer   Date

Figure 7.7   Code violation notification

Your Company Name
Your Company Address
Your Company Phone and Fax Numbers

CERTIFICATE OF COMPLETION
AND ACCEPTANCE

Contractor: _____

Customer: _____

Job name: _____

Job location: _____

Job description: _____

_____

_____

Date of completion: _____

Date of final inspection by customer: _____

Date of code compliance inspection and approval: _____

Defects found in material or workmanship: _____

_____

_____

_____

ACKNOWLEDGMENT

Customer acknowledges the completion of all contracted work and accepts all workmanship and materials as being satisfactory. Upon signing this certificate, the customer releases the contractor from any responsibility for additional work, except warranty work. Warranty work will be performed for a period of _____ from the date of completion. Warranty work will include the repair of any material or workmanship defects occurring between now and the end of the warranty period. All existing workmanship and materials are acceptable to the customer and payment will be made, in full, according to the payment schedule in the contract, between the two parties.

_____   _____
Customer   Date   Contractor   Date

Figure 7.8 Certificate of completion and acceptance

Considerations for Evaluating a Project				
Consideration	**Applies**	**Does Not Apply**	**Is Satisfactory**	**Is Not Satisfactory**
Time needed for project development				
Location of project				
Demographics				
Zoning				
Setbacks				
Deed restrictions				
Wetlands				
Erosion potential				
Hazardous materials				
Environmental scan				
Soils studies				
Comparable properties				
Schools				
Shopping				
Public transportation				
Local housing				
Employment opportunities				
Traffic count				
Recreational opportunities				
Code requirements				
Is the site in a historic district?				
Comparable sales				
Present real estate market conditions				
Projected real estate market conditions				

Checklist 7.1   Considerations for evaluating a project

COST PROJECTIONS

Item/Phase	Labor	Material	Total
Total estimated expense			

Figure 7.9 Cost projections

Your Company Name
Your Company Address
Your Company Phone and Fax Numbers

DEMAND FOR DELIVERY

Date: _____

To (Supplier): _____

_____

_____

The Undersigned has paid you $_____ for goods to be shipped pursuant to our accepted order dated _____, 19_____; and we therefore demand delivery of said goods in accordance with our order.

Unless these goods are received by us on or before _____, 19 _____, we shall consider you in breach and demand full refund, reserving all other rights under the Uniform Commercial Code.

Please notify us of your intentions.

Sincerely,

_____

Title: _____

Figure 7.10   Demand for delivery

FIELD EXPENSES

Expenses	Amount
Vehicles	
Vehicle maintenance	
Fuel	
Mobile communications	
Field supervisors	
Equipment	
Signs	
Supplies	
Total	

Figure 7.11   Field expenses

INSPECTION LOG

Phase	Ordered	Approved

Figure 7.12 Inspection log

Your Company Name
Your Company Address
Your Company Phone and Fax Numbers

LOST/STOLEN EQUIPMENT REPORT

Date of report:_____

Date of loss:_____

Time of loss (when was item last seen):_____

Location of loss:_____

Type of item lost/stolen (include serial number):_____

_____

Item was lost / stolen (circle appropriate word)

Name of person in charge of equipment at time of

loss:_____

Was notification given to the police?:_____

Additional comments: _____

_____

_____

_____

_____

_____

_____

_____

Figure 7.13 Lost/stolen equipment report

VEHICLE-RELATED EXPENSES

Date	Type	Amount	Driver	Form of Payment

Figure 7.14 Vehicle mileage log

OFFICE EXPENSES

Expense	Amount
Rent	
Utilities	
Phone service	
Answering service	
Office cleaning	
Equipment rentals	
Furniture	
Supplies	
Total	

Figure 7.15 Office expenses

MATERIAL ORDER LOG

Supplier: _____

Date   order   was   placed:

_____

Time order was placed: _____

Name of person taking order: _____

Promised delivery date: _____

Order   number:

_____

Quoted price: _____

Date of follow-up call: _____

Manager's name: _____

Time of call to manager: _____

Manager confirmed delivery date: _____

Manager confirmed price: _____

Notes and comments: _____

_____

_____

_____

_____

_____

_____

_____

_____

Figure 7.16 Material order log

Your Company Name
Your Company Address
Your Company Phone and Fax Numbers

REJECTION OF GOODS

Date: _____

To: _____

_____

_____

We received goods from you under our order or contract dated _____, 19 _____.
However, we reject said goods for the reason(s) checked below:

_____ Goods failed to be delivered within the required contract time.

_____ Goods were defective or damaged as described on attached sheet.

_____ Goods did not conform to sample or specifications as described on attached sheet.
_____ Confirmation accepting our order, as required, has not been received, and we
therefore ordered the goods from another supplier.

_____ Prices for said goods do not conform to quote, catalogue, or purchase order price.

_____ Partial shipment only received; we do not accept partial shipments.

_____ Other (please see attached sheet).

Please provide instructions for return of said goods at your expense. Rejection of said
goods shall not waive any other claim we may have.

Sincerely,

_____

Title: _____

Figure 7.17 Rejection of goods

Your Company Name
Your Company Address
Your Company Phone and Fax Numbers

PAYMENT ON SPECIFIC ACCOUNTS

Date: _____

To: _____

_____

_____

Our enclosed check number _____ for $_____ should be credited to the following charges or invoices only:

Invoice/Debt	Amount
	$

Payments herein shall be applied only to those specified items listed and shall not be applied, in whole or in part, to other obligations.

Sincerely,

_____

Title: _____

Figure 7.18   Payment on specific accounts

Your Company Name
Your Company Address
Your Company Phone and Fax Numbers

LETTER SOLICITING MATERIAL QUOTES

Date:

Dear:

I am soliciting bids for the work listed below, and I would like to offer you the opportunity to participate in the bidding. If you are interested in giving quoted prices on material(s) for this job, please let me hear from you at the above address.

The job will be started in _____ days/weeks. Financing has been arranged and the job will be started on schedule. Your quote, if you choose to enter one, must be received no later than _____.

The proposed work is as follows: _____ _____ _____

Plans and specifications for the work are available upon request.

Thank you for your time and consideration in this request.

Sincerely,

Your Name
Title

Figure 7.19 Letter soliciting material quotes

TAKE-OFF FORM

Job name: _____

Job address: _____

Item	Quantity	Description

Figure 7.20   Take-off form

VEHICLE-RELATED EXPENSES

Date	Type	Amount	Driver	Form of Payment

Figure 7.21 Vehicle-related expenses

PMB #300 13 Gurnet Road
Brunswick, Maine 04011

Phone: 207-729-8375
Fax: 207-798-5070
Email: tmg1@mfx.net

The Masters Group, Inc.

Fax

To:	R. E. Green	**From:**	Roger Woodson
Fax:	207-798-5070 (TMG)	**Pages:**	2
Phone:	207-666-8254 (TMG)	**Date:**	2/17/2004
Re:	Classified ads	**CC:**	

Dear Mr. Green,

The page following this one has small classified ads that I would like to place as soon as possible in the Real Estate Wanted section of the classifieds. I would also like to talk with you about additional ads. I can be reached at 666-8254 today and much of tomorrow.

Thank you.

Roger Woodson

Figure 7.22 Professional fax cover letter

Company Name
Your Company Address
Your Company Phone and Fax Numbers

WEEKLY EXPENSE REPORT

Employee name: _____   Department: _____

Office   location/extension: _____   Week   ending:

_____

TRANSPORTATION	Sun.	Mon.	Tues.	Wed.	Thurs.	Fri.	Sat.	TOTAL
Total automobile miles x mileage rate .20								
Gas, oil, maintenance								
Parking and tolls								
Auto rental								
Taxi								
Other (air, rail, bus)								
TOTAL TRANSPORTATION								
MEALS AND LODGING								
Hotel (include parking, tips)								
Breakfast								
Lunch								
Dinner								
Other Meals								
TOTAL MEALS AND LODGING								
MISCELLANEOUS								
Laundry, cleaning								
Phone, fax								
Sundries								
Entertainment (detail below)								
TOTAL MISCELLANEOUS								
PER DAY TOTALS								

Total expenses   _____
Less cash advance and charges to Company   _____
Amount due me (Company) $ _____

Entertainment Details

Date	Event	Clients Entertained	Location	Business Purpose	Amount

Signature: _____   Title: _____   Date: _____

Approval: _____   Title: _____   Date: _____

Figure 7.23   Weekly expense report

ACCOUNTS RECEIVABLE LOG

Date	Account Description	Amount Due	Date Due	Date Received

Figure 7.23 Accounts receivable log